AUTODESK® MAYA® 2014

ESSENTIALS

AUTODESK® MAYA® 2014
ESSENTIALS

Paul Naas

AUTODESK.
Official Press

SYBEX®
A Wiley Brand

Acquisitions Editor: Mariann Barsolo
Development Editor: Kim Beaudet
Technical Editor: Jon McFarland
Production Editor: Christine O'Connor
Copy Editor: Tiffany Taylor
Editorial Manager: Pete Gaughan
Production Manager: Tim Tate
Vice President and Executive Group Publisher: Richard Swadley
Vice President and Publisher: Neil Edde
Book Designer: Happenstance Type-O-Rama
Compositor: Cody Gates, Happenstance Type-O-Rama
Proofreader: Daniel Aull, Word One New York
Indexer: Nancy Guenther
Project Coordinator, Cover: Katherine Crocker
Cover Designer: Ryan Sneed
Cover Image: Paul Naas

Copyright © 2013 by John Wiley & Sons, Inc., Indianapolis, Indiana
Published simultaneously in Canada
ISBN: 978-1-118-57507-9
ISBN: 978-1-118-74443-7 (ebk.)
ISBN: 978-1-118-75032-2 (ebk.)
ISBN: 978-1-118-74437-6 (ebk.)

For general information on our other products and services or to obtain technical support, please contact our Customer Care Department within the U.S. at (877) 762-2974, outside the U.S. at (317) 572-3993 or fax (317) 572-4002.

Library of Congress Control Number: 2013935676

Dear Reader,

Thank you for choosing *Autodesk Maya 2014 Essentials*. This book is part of a family of premium-quality Sybex books, all of which are written by outstanding authors who combine practical experience with a gift for teaching.

Sybex was founded in 1976. More than 30 years later, we're still committed to producing consistently exceptional books. With each of our titles, we're working hard to set a new standard for the industry. From the paper we print on, to the authors we work with, our goal is to bring you the best books available.

I hope you see all that reflected in these pages. I'd be very interested to hear your comments and get your feedback on how we're doing. Feel free to let me know what you think about this or any other Sybex book by sending me an email at nedde@wiley.com. If you think you've found a technical error in this book, please visit http://sybex.custhelp.com. Customer feedback is critical to our efforts at Sybex.

Best regards,

Neil Edde
Vice President and Publisher
Sybex, an Imprint of Wiley

To everyone I've worked with, I've learned from, and has encouraged me over the years, thanks for your support. I do what I love every day thanks to you.

And to my students, who keep me on my toes and teach me things every day without ever realizing it.
Now go do your homework!

Acknowledgments

A couple of years ago at SIGGRAPH, I was trying to find a book to use as a textbook for an Introduction to 3D class I was teaching. I hit every publisher's booth, complaining to anyone who would listen that there wasn't a good, basic, introductory book for learning Autodesk® Maya® software. In the Wiley/Sybex booth, Mariann Barsolo listened to my whining and then simply said, "Why don't you write one?" The end result of that brief (but certainly not final) conversation is the book you hold in your hands. My thanks to Mariann for giving me this terrific opportunity.

Thanks also go to the editing team at Wiley: Kim Beaudet, Pete Gaughan, Christine O'Connor, Tiffany Taylor, and Jon McFarland. I may have typed the words into the computer, but they made sure it all made sense.

None of this would have been possible without the support and encouragement of the staff and faculty of Cañada College. I am especially grateful to our Vice President of Instruction Linda Hayes, my dean Jan Roecks, and our division office staff Jonna Pounds and Peter Tam. I can never fully express my gratitude for how you all made this easier for me.

ABOUT THE AUTHOR

 **Paul Naas is an** associate professor and coordinator for the Multimedia Arts & Technology department at Cañada College in Redwood City, California. Trained as a traditional animator, Paul got some early professional experience while still in college, working on station IDs for MTV. He transitioned into CG in 1994 with his first job in the video game industry, working on 3D Studio DOS. Later he became one of the first animators hired at the Disney Institute in Orlando, Florida, where he taught animation, character design, animation history, and voice-over. Over the course of his nearly 20-year career, Paul has worked on independent films, TV spots, video games, e-learning projects, location-based entertainment, and mobile-device applications. Paul holds a Master of Fine Arts degree in animation from Academy of Art University, San Francisco, California.

CONTENTS AT A GLANCE

CONTENTS

CHAPTER 7   **Getting Bent Out of Shape: Blend Shapes**   **135**

CHAPTER 8   **Dem Bones: Setting Up Your Joint System**   **147**

CHAPTER 9   **Weighting Your Joints**   **173**

CHAPTER 13   Let There Be Light: Lighting Your Shot   237

CHAPTER 14   Rendering and Compositing Your Scene   255

APPENDIX A   Autodesk® Maya® 2014 Certification   269

INTRODUCTION

Welcome to Autodesk® Maya® 2014 Essentials. Autodesk® Maya® software is one of many 3D computer graphics (CG) packages available on the market, and although it has many unique features, it shares one trait with every other package out there: it's very powerful and very complex. The goal of this book is to walk you through some of the features of the software and familiarize you with the tools Maya provides and how to use them.

Although nearly every chapter in this book provides a tutorial that covers a particular facet of the software, the goal is not to show you how to do one single procedure. In every case, the intent is to provide you with background and context for the steps you're performing, so that you develop an understanding of the procedure and its place within the overall CG workflow and can apply that knowledge to all your future projects. In many cases, the tutorials provided take you step by step through an entire process, ending with a specific result. In other chapters, while there are still step-by-step instructions provided, it would be impossible to take you through the entire procedure. In these cases, the information presented is more conceptual and explains the "why" of what you're doing, rather than the "what."

With that end in mind, the tutorials in this book are designed to be comprehensive but as simple as possible to complete. Many books on CG provide tutorials that are too complex, frustrating readers and leaving them with more questions than answers. The results of the tutorials in this book may look simple, but the process of completing them will give you a solid foundation in creating CG imagery.

That said, you will probably make some mistakes along the way. That's simply part of the learning process. If it happens, just try again. After all, you don't learn to drive a car by hopping on the freeway or entering the Daytona 500—you start out in a parking lot where there is lots of room for error. I tell my students that if they have to redo a procedure, they'll find that the second time around it'll go faster and the results will be better—and that has always been the case.

Who Should Read This Book

Anyone who wants to learn how to use Maya should start learning with this book. The exercises are organized like a production would be, moving from preproduction tasks (modeling, rigging) through production (animation), and finally postproduction (lighting, rendering, compositing). In addition to mimicking the structure of a game or film production, the exercises here are designed to expose you to the process of creating CG while being as easy to complete as possible. Many books try to cram too much into their tutorials, confusing and frustrating readers in the process. The goal of *Autodesk® Maya® 2014 Essentials* is to give you a solid foundation in the software so you can explore the areas that most interest you in further detail.

What You Will Learn

This book covers the fundamentals of working in CG with Maya. It's only a starting point, though. As with any artistic pursuit, CG is a lifelong process of learning. With what you learn in this book forming a solid foundation, you can continue exploring all the complex, interesting facets of creating CG imagery. And I promise you that by the end of this book, you'll never watch a CG animated film or an effects-laden summer blockbuster the same way again.

What You Need

As with any CG software, Maya requires a significant amount of computing power to run smoothly and efficiently. A good rule of thumb for Maya (or any 3D software) is to run it on a computer with the fastest processor, the most RAM, and the best video card you can get your hands on. At a minimum, you need 4 GB of RAM, 10 GB of hard drive space, and a qualified hardware-accelerated OpenGL graphics card. Maya runs on Windows, Mac, and Linux systems. For details on system specifications and qualified graphics cards, go to `http://www.autodesk.com/products/autodesk-maya/overview` and click on the System Requirements link.

This book is a great primer for Autodesk Maya. If you're interested in taking the Autodesk Certification exams for Maya, go to www.autodesk.com/ certification for information and resources.

FREE AUTODESK SOFTWARE FOR STUDENTS AND EDUCATORS

The Autodesk Education Community is an online resource with more than five million members that enables educators and students to download—for free (see website for terms and conditions)—the same software used by professionals worldwide. You can also access additional tools and materials to help you design, visualize, and simulate ideas. Connect with other learners to stay current with the latest industry trends and get the most out of your designs. Get started today at www.autodesk.com/joinedu.

What Is Covered in This Book

As mentioned earlier, the bulk of this book is organized like a production, with the chapters proceeding through the process of creating and animating a character similar to how that process would take place when developing a game or film project.

Chapter 1: Understanding the Maya Interface   This chapter is a quick and thorough introduction to the interface elements you'll work with throughout the rest of the book. It also serves as a great reference as you progress through the exercises that follow.

Chapter 2: Creating Your First Animation   This chapter provides a fun way to get started exploring Maya. When you're finished, you'll have a short animation of a bouncing ball that uses several Maya tools, as well as a number of principles of animation.

Chapter 3: Modeling with Polygons, Part 1   This chapter starts your travels through a production flow by having you rough out the overall shape of a character. You'll block in the basic shapes and begin the modeling process.

Chapter 4: Modeling with Polygons, Part 2   Building on what you did in the previous chapter, in this chapter you'll add details and continue the modeling process, getting the majority of the character built.

Chapter 5: Modeling with Polygons, Part 3   Here you'll put the finishing touches on your character, perform some cleanup tasks, and prepare the model for rigging.

Chapter 6: Surfacing Your Character   Laying out the UVs of your character is a critical step in the production process that lets you use texture maps for color and detail. This chapter shows you how to lay out UV maps and create textures and surface shaders.

Chapter 7: Getting Bent Out of Shape: Blend Shapes   Facial expressions are at the heart of every good piece of character animation. In this chapter, you'll create deformers that allow you to create facial expressions on your character.

Chapter 8: Dem Bones: Setting Up Your Joint System   Character models require joint systems that allow you to pose the model. This chapter walks you through the process of building a skeleton that will create the overall body deformations necessary to animate your character.

Chapter 9: Weighting Your Joints   This chapter describes and demonstrates the process of joint weighting, which is critical to creating smooth, pleasing deformations when your character's skeleton is manipulated.

Chapter 10: Rigging Your Character   Every good rig has controls that make it faster and easier to animate. In this chapter, you'll set up control structures that allow you to animate your character quickly and easily.

Chapter 11: Setting the Scene: Creating an Environment   A character needs a space in which to perform. This chapter takes you through the process of creating a set and making some simple props and set dressing, and gives you a little more practice creating shaders and applying them to geometry.

Chapter 12: Making It Move: Animating Your Character   This chapter takes you step by step through animating your character performing a simple action. You pose your character, set keyframes, and make adjustments that bring your character to life.

Chapter 13: Let There Be Light: Lighting Your Shot   Good lighting can completely change the mood and meaning of a scene. This chapter describes the three-point lighting system and takes you through the process of setting one up in your scene.

Chapter 14: Rendering and Compositing Your Scene   After all your work, you're going to want to show your shot to family and friends. This chapter walks you through generating final output from your scene and compiling it into a QuickTime movie.

Appendix: Autodesk Maya 2014 Certification   This appendix contains the objectives to the Autodesk Maya 2014 Certified Professional Exam and a table that lists the topic, exam objective, and chapter where the information can be found.

 N O T E   Go to www.autodesk.com/certification to find information about the Maya 2014 Certified Professional exam covered in this book, as well as other Maya certification exams.

The Essentials Series

The Essentials series from Sybex provides outstanding instructions for readers who are just beginning to develop their professional skills. Every Essentials book includes these features:

▶ Skill-based instruction with chapters organized around projects rather than abstract concepts or subjects.

▶ Suggestions for additional exercises at the end of each chapter, where you can practice and extend your skills.

▶ Digital files (via download) so you can work through the project tutorials yourself. Please check the book's web page at www.sybex.com/go/maya2014essentials for these companion downloads.

You can contact the author through Wiley or on Facebook at www.facebook.com/MayaEssentials. I hope you have fun with the material that follows.

CHAPTER 1

Understanding the Maya Interface

Before you start creating in the Autodesk® Maya® program, it's a good idea to familiarize yourself with the application's interface and the tools you'll need to use frequently. The Maya interface can be intimidating and confusing, but you can start by getting to know a few of the windows and tools, and then learn the rest as necessary. This chapter presents what you need to know to get started.

▶ **Exploring interface elements**

▶ **Moving views and manipulating objects**

▶ **Using windows and menus**

▶ **Setting preferences**

▶ **Getting help**

Exploring Interface Elements

The appearance of the interface windows on your machine may vary from the images in this book, depending on the operating system you're using.

On first glance, understanding Maya's interface can seem to be a daunting task (see Figure 1.1).

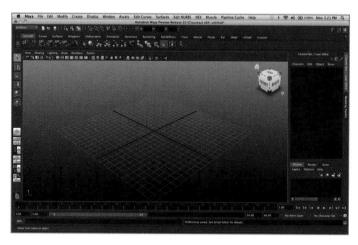

FIGURE 1.1   The Maya interface

Fortunately, you don't need to know what all those buttons and icons do right now. In fact, you can spend years working in Maya and never touch some of those buttons, depending on the kind of work you do. That said, you'll use several of these buttons, windows, and menus frequently and so you should be familiar with them.

One of the best ways to become familiar with the common tools in Maya is to take a look at some of the extensive Help files Maya has available—specifically, the 1-Minute Startup Movies. Choose Help ➢ 1-Minute Startup Movies, and view the first five movies. We'll get into the topics covered by movies 6 and 7 later. Go ahead, watch the movies; I'll wait.

Back already? Great—now you have a little information about some of the common tools, menus, and commands in Maya. Let's explore them in a bit more detail.

Views

When you start a new Maya scene, the *Perspective view* opens by default. In 3D, it's often important to see your scene from more than one view, and it's easy to do that in Maya. Figure 1.2 shows the default Maya window.

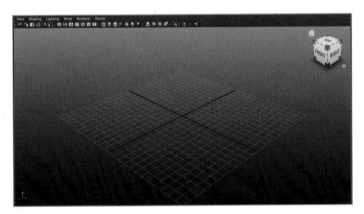

FIGURE 1.2 Default Maya window

To see multiple views, place your cursor in the Perspective view and tap the spacebar. The single-view window becomes a four-view window with Front, Side, and Top views in addition to the Perspective view you started with. To return to a single view, place your cursor in the view you want to be displayed full-screen and tap the spacebar again. Any of the four views can be displayed full-screen, as well as several other types of views we'll discuss later.

Time Slider

At the bottom of the screen below the view window is the *Time Slider*, shown in Figure 1.3. The Time Slider shows the range of frames that are currently active in the scene, the location of the playback head, and the frames that have keyframes set on them for any selected object. (Keyframes are frames on which you specify actions, such as movement or rotation, for specific objects. Keyframes are discussed in detail in Chapter 12, "Making It Move: Animating Your Character.")

Playback Head   Time Slider

FIGURE 1.3 Time Slider

Try moving the playback head around. You can either click a frame to move the playback head to that position, or click and drag the head to move it.

Range Slider

Below the Time Slider is the Range Slider. The *Range Slider* shows the total number of frames currently in the scene, and the portion of those frames that are currently active. To the left of the Range Slider are two windows containing information about the first frame of the scene and the first frame of the currently active frame range. To the right of the Range Slider are two windows containing information about the last frame of the currently active frame range and the last frame of the scene. Figure 1.4 shows the Range Slider and the frame windows.

Beginning
of Scene

Range Slider

End of Active Scene

Beginning of
Active Range

End of Scene

FIGURE 1.4   Range Slider

Try changing the length of the active range. One way is to click the square button on the right side of the Range Slider and drag left or right.

Toolbox Window

On the left side of the screen is the *Toolbox window*, shown in Figure 1.5. The Toolbox contains buttons for many of the commonly used tools in Maya, as well as a space that contains the most recently used tool.

FIGURE 1.5
Toolbox window

Shelves

Above the view window is a nifty little group of icons called a *shelf*. Maya comes with several default shelves, such as polygonal modeling, animation, and rendering shelves. What's really handy, though, is that you can create your own custom shelves and populate them with the tools you use most frequently. The default shelves and any custom shelves you create are accessible via the tab on the left side of the shelf or by the tabs that are just above the shelf icons. Figure 1.6 shows a shelf and the tabs.

FIGURE 1.6   Shelf

Moving Views and Manipulating Objects

Within the Maya 3D space, you can move your position, manipulate an object, or both. The first descriptions in the following list are of the view tools, followed by the tools that enable you to move, rotate, and scale objects:

Tumble   Tumbling the view enables you to rotate around objects in the scene. The Tumble tool works only in Perspective views. The keyboard combination for tumbling is Option/Alt + left mouse button (LMB). Figure 1.7 shows this keyboard/mouse combination.

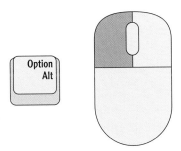

FIGURE 1.7   Tumble keyboard/mouse combination

Pan   Panning the view enables you to move side to side and up and down within a view. The keyboard combination for panning is Option/Alt + middle mouse button (MMB). In most cases, the MMB is your mouse's scroll wheel. Figure 1.8 shows this keyboard/mouse combination.

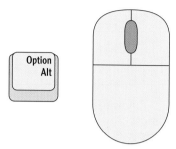

FIGURE 1.8   Pan keyboard/mouse combination

Zoom   Zooming the view enables you to move closer to or farther away from objects in the scene. The keyboard combination for zooming is Option/Alt + right mouse button (RMB). Figure 1.9 shows this keyboard/mouse combination.

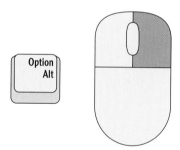

FIGURE 1.9   Zoom keyboard/mouse combination

Other Zooming Options   Maya also has a couple of keyboard commands that zoom in on objects in the scene:

▶ Press the a key to zoom in to show every visible object in the scene.

▶ Press the f key to zoom in to show every selected object in the scene. If nothing is selected, the f key behaves like the a key.

The ViewCube   Another way to navigate within a view window is with the ViewCube, shown in Figure 1.10. You can manipulate the view by clicking and dragging the cube, by clicking a cube face or edge, or by clicking the Home icon above and to the left of the cube, which returns you to the standard view for that window. Try manipulating the view with the ViewCube.

FIGURE 1.10
ViewCube

Move Tool   The Move tool can be accessed by clicking its button in the Toolbox (shown in Figure 1.11) or by pressing w on your keyboard. This tool enables you to move an object anywhere in the scene. Clicking and dragging one of the colored handles constrains the motion to that one axis, whereas clicking and dragging the center where the three handles meet allows you to move along more than one axis. Create a polygon sphere by clicking Create ➢ Polygon Primitives ➢ Sphere and then dragging in the view (if a sphere didn't automatically appear). Select the Move tool, and move your sphere around.

—Move Tool
—Rotate Tool
—Scale Tool

FIGURE 1.11
Move, Rotate, and Scale tools

Rotate Tool   The Rotate tool, shown in Figure 1.11, can be selected by clicking its button in the Toolbox window or by pressing e. The red, green, and blue handles surrounding the object constrain the rotation to one axis, and the larger circle outside of them rotates the object parallel to the view plane. Try rotating your sphere around one or more axes. The small circle inside the red, green, and blue circles is used for free rotation on all three axes.

Scale Tool   The Scale tool enables you to change the size of your object. To access the tool, you can click the button, shown in Figure 1.11, or press r. The object's handles look similar to the Move handles, but the Scale handles have cubes on their ends. As with the Move tool, dragging a single handle constrains the scaling to that axis, whereas dragging the center where the three handles meet scales on all three axes at the same time. Try scaling your sphere, both on a single axis and as a whole object.

Enlarging or Reducing the Manipulator Handles   Sometimes the manipulator handles for Move, Rotate, and Scale are either too long or too short to work with. Adjusting their length is easy. With one of the tools active, press the Plus key (+) to lengthen (or, in the case of Rotate, enlarge) the handles, or press the Minus key (-) to shorten (or shrink) the handles. Select your sphere, and practice lengthening and shortening the manipulator handles.

Using Maya Windows and Menus

There are several windows and menus in Maya that you'll use frequently. Some are always available to you, and others are brought up by keyboard commands or mouse clicks:

Channel Box/Layer Editor   The Channel Box/Layer Editor, which is on the right side of the Maya interface, contains information about the object currently selected, such as its position, scale, and modeling history, or other attributes that have been created. If the Channel Box/Layer Editor isn't visible, bring it up by clicking its button in the upper-right corner of the Maya interface. Figure 1.12 shows the Channel Box/Layer Editor.

FIGURE 1.12
Channel Box/Layer Editor

Marking Menu The marking menu, shown in Figure 1.13, allows you to select various attributes of an object, such as edges or faces on a polygon object, or isoparms on a NURBS object. Access the marking menu by right-clicking an object in the scene and continuing to hold the RMB.

FIGURE 1.13 Marking menu

Hotbox The Hotbox is a way to access the menus across the top of the Maya interface without mousing all the way to the top of the window. It contains not only the main menu items but also several other menus that otherwise would be visible only by changing menu sets on the interface. To access the Hotbox, shown in Figure 1.14, place your cursor in the view window and press and hold the spacebar.

FIGURE 1.14 Hotbox

Option Boxes　Sometimes, menu items in Maya have options associated with them that allow you to specify exactly how you want the menu item applied to the object you're working on. You can access these options via the option box that is immediately to the right of the menu item, as shown in Figure 1.15. Not every menu item has an associated option box.

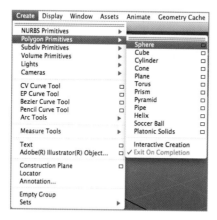

FIGURE 1.15　Option box

To familiarize yourself with using the option box, pick any menu item that has associated options, and click the option box. The Tool Settings window opens, and you can see the various options available for that menu item. Click Cancel (or Close in Windows) to close the window.

Setting Preferences

Maya enables you to customize the interface in several ways. One of the most common is by changing preferences on frequently used features to complement the way you like to work.

Preferences Window

Click the small, square button to the right of the key icon in the bottom-right corner of the interface (shown in Figure 1.16) to open the Maya Preferences window. You can also access the window by choosing Window ➤ Settings/Preferences ➤ Preferences, as shown in Figure 1.17, or by using the Hotbox and selecting the same path.

— Preferences
  Button

FIGURE 1.16 Preferences button

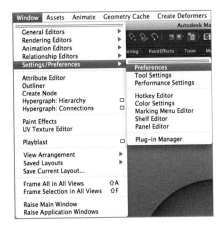

FIGURE 1.17 Preferences menu

The Preferences window is organized into categories that are listed on its left side. Under each category are subcategories. Both the categories and subcategories have options you can set. Selecting one of these categories or subcategories changes the options available to you on the right side of the window. Sometimes it takes a little searching to find what you're looking for, but generally things are pretty well organized and under categories that make sense. Figure 1.18 shows the Preferences window.

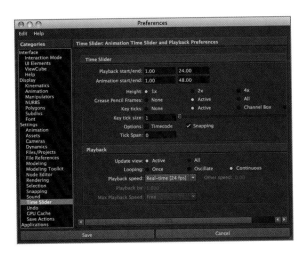

FIGURE 1.18 Preferences window

Settings Used for the Tutorials

Everyone has their favorite tool and display settings for using Maya, and I'm no exception. I prefer to set up Maya so elements are easy to see and I can tell at a glance what I'm doing. I also like to set things up so that I can make as few mistakes as possible if I'm not paying close attention. The following list details a few settings I prefer to use. You're welcome to set your preferences the same way—or not. It's up to you. I'd strongly recommend these settings if you're brand new to Maya, though. They make things much easier to see and make it much harder to make unintended mistakes:

Background   In the Preferences window, select Display on the left side, and then scroll down to the View section on the right. Find Background Gradient, and set it to Off. This gives you a medium-gray background rather than the default gradient—much easier to see what you're doing, in my opinion.

Polygon Selection   Again in the Preferences window, select the Selection subcategory under the Settings category, and then scroll down to the Polygon Selection section on the right side. Choose the option marked Select Faces With: Center. This does a couple of things for you: it makes it harder to accidentally select a polygon when you don't mean to, and it turns on small squares in the center of each poly, which will come in handy when you're modeling.

Playback Speed   Finally, once more in the Preferences window, choose Settings ➤ Time Slider. In the Playback section, set Playback Speed to Real-Time [24 fps]. Click the Save button to save your changes.

Getting Help

As you might expect, loads of resources are available to help you become better at working with Maya. There are many books, magazines, videos, websites, and all sorts of other resources to aid you. Here are a few to get you started:

1-Minute Startup Movies   You've already looked at these once, but don't hesitate to go back and take another look at them if you're unclear on how to do something in the Maya interface. Frequently they're the quickest and most straightforward way to refresh your memory on the basics. You can access the Essential Skills Movies under Help ➤ 1-Minute Startup Movies, as shown in Figure 1.19.

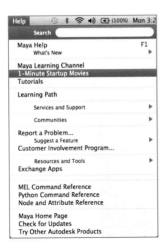

FIGURE 1.19 1-Minute
Startup Movies

Help Files The Help files included with Maya are extensive, searchable, and detailed. You can find basic information about a tool or detailed tutorials to help you master a technique. The Help files are organized and searchable via the table of contents or the index. You can access the Help files under Help ➢ Maya Help, as shown in Figure 1.20.

FIGURE 1.20 Maya Help files

Area Website   Autodesk has an online community website called Area where you can browse the topics being discussed or post a question. A screenshot of Area is shown in Figure 1.21. In addition, tutorials, free downloads, and more are available to inspire you and help you get up to speed. Membership is required, but registration is free. Joining Area is highly recommended. The URL is http://area.autodesk.com/.

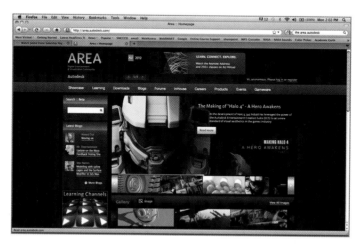

FIGURE 1.21   Area website

The Essentials and Beyond

The Maya interface can be daunting, with all its buttons and menus. Now you have a working knowledge of some of the parts of that interface, and you can get started in Maya.

Additional Exercises

▶ Change menu sets by using the drop-down window in the upper-left corner of the interface, and observe how some of the menu options across the top of the screen change.

▶ Switch the shelf that's on display, and hover over some of the icons on the new shelf to see what tool the button calls up. (Some of the icons are pretty abstract.)

CHAPTER 2

Creating Your First Animation

Autodesk® Maya® software can be used for many steps in a production, but one of the most fun—both to play around with and show to friends and family—is animation. So you'll start out by creating a simple animation. The clip you're going to produce is one of the first exercises any animator completes: the bouncing ball.

▶ **Using good scene-file management**

▶ **Creating and animating a bouncing ball**

▶ **Refining movement in the Graph Editor**

▶ **Using animation principles to improve your work**

▶ **Creating a playblast of your animation**

Using Good Scene-File Management

Before you start, you need to set up your Maya scene so all of your assets are organized and easy to find. This will be very important as you work on more complex projects, so it's a good habit to get into right from the start.

Maya provides a way to easily keep all the files for a project organized. It's called the *project directory*. Every time you start a new scene, you should set up a new project directory by following these steps:

1. Choose File ➤ New Scene.

2. Choose File ➢ Project Window. The Project window opens, as shown in Figure 2.1.

FIGURE 2.1 Project window

3. Click the New button next to the Current Project field, and give your project a unique name such as Project1 or BouncingBall, as shown in Figure 2.2.

FIGURE 2.2 Project name

4. Confirm that your project is being saved to the maya/projects directory by checking the Location field, shown in Figure 2.3.

FIGURE 2.3   Checking the project location

Maya creates subdirectories within your main directory to hold various scene elements. These are listed under Primary Project Locations, as shown in Figure 2.4.

Subdirectories

FIGURE 2.4   Project subdirectories

5. Click the Accept button to close the Project window.

6. Finally, make sure your scene has 24 active frames by checking the Time Slider, as shown in Figure 2.5. If you don't have 24 frames, adjust the length of the Range Slider or type 24 in the End Time window.

Range Slider Adjustment   End Time Window

FIGURE 2.5   Setting the scene to 24 frames

Creating and Animating a Bouncing Ball

Before you start animating, you're going to change your view and turn on an option that will let you see exactly the space you're working in. Then you'll create your ball and set the keys that will get it bouncing.

Selecting a View and Turning On the Resolution Gate

To make it easier to animate your ball, you'll work in the Front view and turn on an option that shows just how much of that window would show up if you were to create a final render of your animation. Follow these steps:

1. Place your cursor in the view window, and tap the spacebar to access the four-view layout.

2. Place your cursor in the Front view, and tap the spacebar to make the Front view active in the single-view layout.

3. In the menu at the top of the view window, choose View ➢ Camera Settings ➢ Resolution Gate, as shown in Figure 2.6.

FIGURE 2.6   Camera Settings menu

A rectangle appears in the Front view. Anything within the rectangle will appear in a final render. Anything in the gray area outside the rectangle won't show up.

4. Using the Pan keyboard/mouse combination (Option/Alt + MMB), move the thick, black line to the bottom of the screen. Your view should look something like Figure 2.7.

Alternatively, you can click the small shaded sphere icon at the top of the Front view to turn on the resolution gate (the icon is visible in Figure 2.6 just to the right of the View menu).

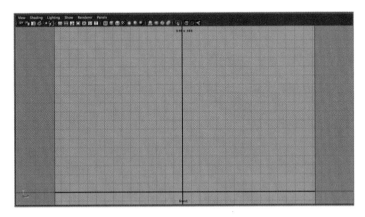

FIGURE 2.7   View setup

Creating a Ball

You'll use a polygon sphere for your bouncing ball. They're easy to work with and look pretty good. Follow these steps to create the ball:

1. Choose Create ➤ Polygon Primitives, and click Interactive Creation to uncheck it, as shown in Figure 2.8.

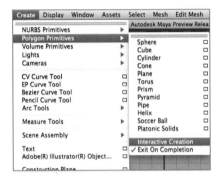

FIGURE 2.8   Turn off Interactive Creation.

2. Choose Create ➢ Polygon Primitives ➢ Sphere ➢ Option Box, and click. Figure 2.9 shows the selection.

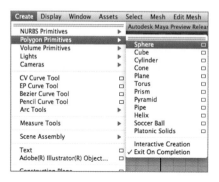

F I G U R E   2 . 9   **Create Polygon Primitives Sphere menu**

3. In the Polygon Sphere Options window, shown in Figure 2.10, set the radius to 2.5.

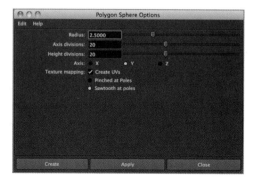

F I G U R E   2 . 1 0   **Polygon Sphere Options window**

4. Click the Create button.

5. Press 5 on your numeric keypad or keyboard to shade the sphere. Figure 2.11 shows the shaded sphere.

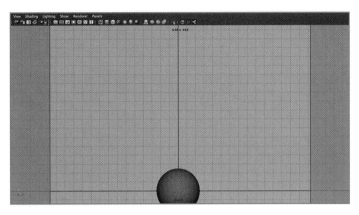

FIGURE 2.11   Your ball, shaded

6. Save your scene, either by choosing File ➢ Save Scene or by pressing
Command/Ctrl + S. Name your scene **bouncingBall** or another name
you choose.

You have your ball; now it's time to bounce it.

Setting Movement Keyframes

To animate in Maya, you set keyframes for various attributes on specific frames.
That lets the software know that on a particular frame, you want a particular attribute to have a particular value. Then Maya interpolates between the keyframes to
create the motion you're after. Let's set some movement keyframes, or keys:

1. Click the Move tool in the Toolbox window (shown in Figure 2.12), or
press w.

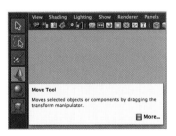

FIGURE 2.12   Move tool

2. Click the sphere, if it's not already selected.

3. Make sure the playback head in the Time Slider is on frame 1, as shown in Figure 2.13.

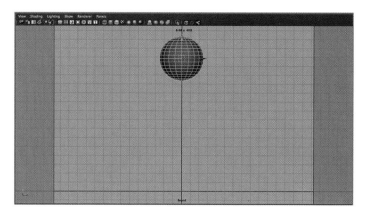

FIGURE 2.13   Playback head

4. Click and hold the green arrowhead on the Move tool, and drag the sphere up to the top of the screen. Release the mouse button. The ball should be positioned similarly to the one in Figure 2.14.

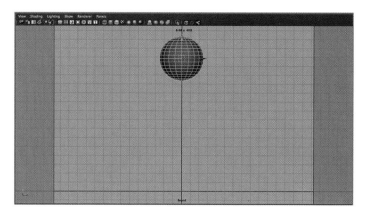

FIGURE 2.14   Initial ball position

5. Press s. This sets a key for the ball's position, rotation, and scale on frame 1. Rotation and scale don't matter currently, just position.

6. Move the playback head to frame 24 by clicking the playback head and dragging, and then press s again. You're creating a *cycle*, and because the ball is already where you want it to end up, you'll just set another key while it's there. Figure 2.15 shows the playback head at frame 24.

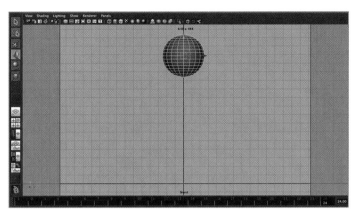

FIGURE 2.15   Setting the final key at frame 24

7. Move the playback head to frame 13.

8. Click the green arrowhead (it will be yellow if still selected) on the Move tool, and drag the sphere down so the bottom just touches the black line. Figure 2.16 shows the ball in its down position.

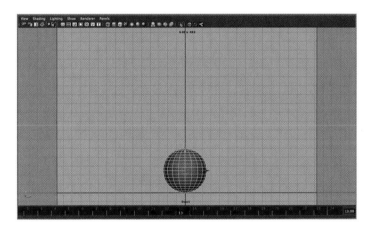

FIGURE 2.16   Moving the ball down

9. Press s to set a key.

10. Save your scene.

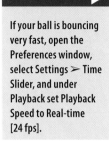

If your ball is bouncing
very fast, open the
Preferences window,
select Settings ➢ Time
Slider, and under
Playback set Playback
Speed to Real-time
[24 fps].

11. Click the Play Forwards button, shown in Figure 2.17, on the lower-right side of the screen to see your ball move.

Play Forwards Button

FIGURE 2.17
Play Forwards button

Refining Movement in the Graph Editor

Your ball is moving—pretty cool! But right now it's not really bouncing. There are a couple of problems with the way it's moving. Part of the task of an animator is to make things move the way you know they should. In this section, you'll adjust some things to get your ball bouncing like a real ball would.

What's Wrong with the Way My Ball Is Bouncing?

The reason the ball is moving the way it is has to do with how Maya tries to interpolate between keys. Maya uses *tangents* to interpolate between the keys you set, and sometimes the tangents don't work as you need them to. Your next step is to adjust the tangents so the ball moves the way you want:

1. Press Esc to stop playback.

2. With the ball still selected, choose Window ➢ Animation Editors ➢ Graph Editor, as shown in Figure 2.18.

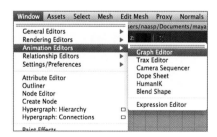

FIGURE 2.18 **Graph Editor menu selection**

3. With pSphere1 selected, press a on your keyboard.

Several lines appear in the Graph Editor window. These are the tangents for the attributes you set by pressing s. You need only one of these, so you'll select just that one.

4. Click Translate Y in the left column of the Graph Editor.

5. Press a on your keyboard to zoom in on the tangent. Your window should look similar to Figure 2.19.

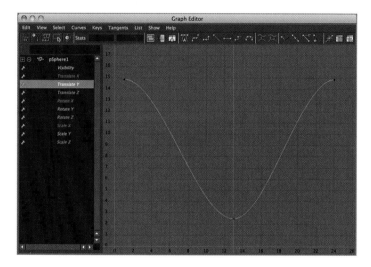

FIGURE 2.19   Translate Y in the Graph Editor

Adjusting Spline Tangents

The tangent tells you a lot about how something's moving. The greater the change in the tangent as it moves from left to right, the faster the change in that attribute onscreen. The smaller the change in the tangent, the slower the change in that attribute. Looking at the tangent for Translate Y, you can see that the ball starts out slowly (as shown by the flat tangent lines), picks up speed (represented by the steep tangent lines), and slows down as it nears and leaves the key at frame 13 (represented by the shallow curve in the tangent). That's pretty much what you saw when you played your animation. Let's adjust the tangents so you get a more believable bounce:

1. Drag-select the keys at frames 1 and 24 (the small, black boxes at the beginning and end of the tangent line). The boxes highlight, and handles appear extending from them, as shown in Figure 2.20.

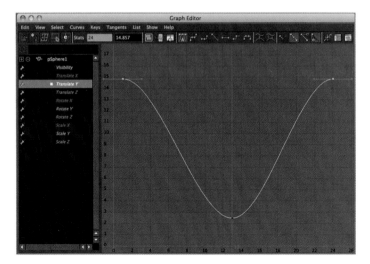

FIGURE 2.20   **Keys selected**

2. The handles should be horizontal, which is how you want them so the ball starts off slowly. If they aren't horizontal, click the Auto Tangents button (the button at the top of the window with an *A* under a tangent line).

3. Save your scene.

Breaking Tangents for Fast Direction Changes

The start and stop look good, but you have to fix the motion of the ball as it hits the "ground." To do this, you're going to break the tangents before and after the key on frame so you can adjust them individually:

1. Drag-select the key at frame 13.

2. Click the Break Tangents button at the top of the Graph Editor window. Figure 2.21 shows the button's location.

Break Tangents Tool

FIGURE 2.21
Break Tangents tool

3. Drag-select the handle on the left side of the key.

4. Left-click anywhere within the Graph Editor window, and drag upward to move the handle. If the handle doesn't move, make sure you have the Move tool selected by pressing w on your keyboard. Adjust the handle so it looks more or less like Figure 2.22.

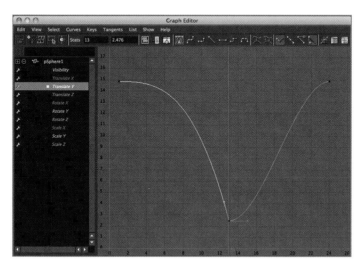

FIGURE 2.22 Adjusting the tangent handle

5. Drag-select the handle on the right side of the key.

6. Left-click anywhere within the Graph Editor window, and drag upward. Adjust the handle so it looks more or less like Figure 2.23.

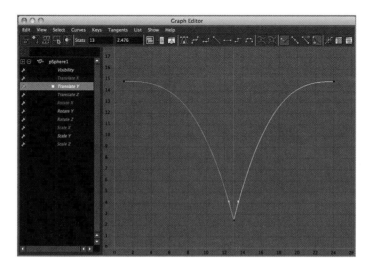

FIGURE 2.23 Adjusting the second tangent handle

7. Close the Graph Editor window.

8. Save your scene.

9. Click the Play Forward button at lower-right on the screen. Your ball should now bounce much more like a regular ball.

Using Animation Principles to Improve Your Work

The ball is bouncing well, but you can add some interest to the cycle by using basic animation principles.

Squash

You'll use a technique called *squash* to give more force to the ball's impact with the ground. Press the Esc key to stop playback, and then follow these steps:

1. Make sure the ball is still selected, and then click frame 12 in the Time Slider to move the playback head there.

2. Press Shift + R. Doing so sets keys just for the scale of your ball.

3. Go to frame 14, and press Shift + R again.

4. Go to frame 13, and enter the following into the scale fields in the Channel Box, as shown in Figure 2.24:

FIGURE 2.24
Channel Box squash values

Scale X: **1.125**

Scale Y: **0.75**

Scale Z: **1.125**

5. Press Return/Enter. Then press Shift + R to set a scale key.

When using squash, it's important to maintain the volume of the object. You don't want the ball to grow or shrink in size, just change shape.

6. Select the Move tool from the Toolbox, or press w on your keyboard.

7. Move the ball back down so the bottom is touching the black line again, as shown in Figure 2.25.

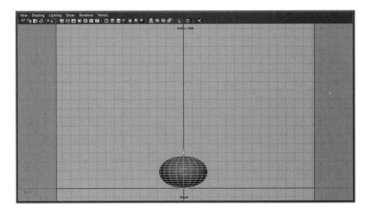

FIGURE 2.25   Squashed ball repositioned

8. Press Shift + W to set a move key for the ball.

9. Save your scene.

10. Click the Play Forwards button, as shown in Figure 2.26.

Play Forwards Button

FIGURE 2.26
Play Forwards button

Your ball now has *squash*. You'll feel it more than see it, and that's how it should be.

Stretch

Squash gave your ball impact with the ground. *Stretch* will give the ball a sense of acceleration and motion blur that happens when objects move fast while being filmed. Press the Esc key to stop playback. Here are the steps for creating stretch:

1. Click frame 7 in the Time Slider to move the playback head there.

2. Press Shift + R to set a scale key.

3. Click frame 18.

4. Press Shift + R.

5. Click frame 12.

6. In the Channel Box, set the following values, as shown in Figure 2.27:

FIGURE 2.27
Channel Box stretch values

Scale X: 0.9

Scale Y: 1.2

Scale Z: 0.9

Just as with squash, you want to maintain the volume of the ball when stretching it. You don't want it to look like it's growing or shrinking.

7. Press Return/Enter, and then press Shift + R to set a scale key. If the end of your ball is extending below the black line, click the green arrow in the ball, move the ball up to a little above the line, and press Shift + W to reset its move key. The ball should look something like Figure 2.28.

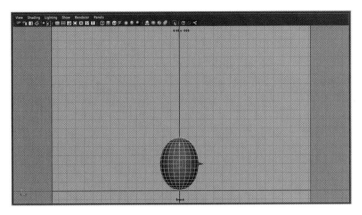

FIGURE 2.28   Stretched ball repositioned

8. Click frame 14, and set the same values.

9. Press Shift + R to set a scale key. Adjust the ball's position if necessary.

10. Save your scene.

11. Click the Play Forwards button.

Your ball now has squash and stretch. Notice how much more flexible and rubbery it looks than it did before.

Creating a Playblast of Your Animation

The Play Forwards button is good for getting a general idea of how your scene looks, but it may not be an accurate example of the speed at which your animation is running. To be sure everything is playing as it should be (as well as to be able to show off your work to others), you're going to make a playblast of your animation. A *playblast* is a low-resolution render that plays as a QuickTime or AVI movie. Follow these steps:

1. Click anywhere in the view window to deselect the ball. The wireframe overlay disappears, leaving you with a gray ball.

2. Choose Window ➢ Playblast ➢ Option Box, as shown in Figure 2.29. The Playblast Options window opens.

FIGURE 2.29 Opening the Playblast Options window

3. Change Scale to 0.50, as shown in Figure 2.30.

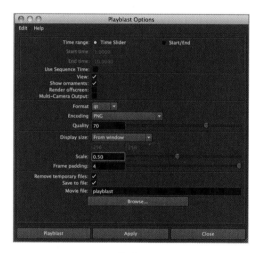

FIGURE 2.30 Scale setting

4. Make sure Save To File is checked, as shown in Figure 2.31. If it isn't, click the check box to select it.

FIGURE 2.31   Save To File setting

5. Under Save To File, click the Browse button and navigate to a location you'll remember (the desktop is usually good).

6. Type in a name for your movie, and click Save.

7. In the Playblast Options window, click the Playblast button, as shown in Figure 2.32.

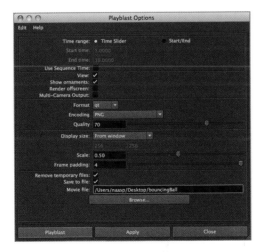

FIGURE 2.32   Playblast button

The playblast renders, and the resulting movie file opens in Apple QuickTime, Microsoft Windows Media Player, or Fcheck, depending on which player is your default.

8. Turn on looping in your player, and then click the Play button.

Congratulations! You've just completed your first 3D animation!

The Essentials and Beyond

In this chapter, you've created your first animated clip. You set keyframes, adjusted tangents in a couple of different ways, worked with movement and scaling, and rendered a playblast movie of your animation.

Additional Exercises

▶ Instead of having the ball bounce straight up and down, how would you bounce it across the screen? Hint: You need only a Translate X key on the first and last frames to make it happen (highlight any Translate X keys in the middle of the tangent and delete them).

▶ Add some more frames to the active frame range, and have your ball bounce more than once. Make each bounce slightly lower than the last, as a real ball would bounce. With the 48 frames you get in a new scene, you should be able to fit in two bounces. If you want to bounce the ball more times, add frames to the scene by typing the number of frames you want in the End Time window below the Time Slider.

▶ If your bounce travels across the screen, turn on Create Editable Motion Trail (Animation menu set, Animate ➢ Create Editable Motion Trail). The motion trail will show you the path your ball is traveling. As your ball moves along the trail, be sure to rotate the stretch keys so the ball looks like it's stretching along the path of travel, as shown in Figure 2.33.

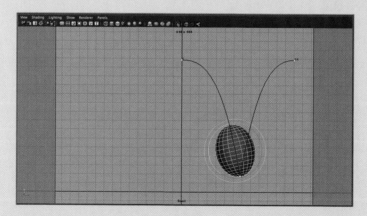

FIGURE 2.33   Squash key rotated

CHAPTER 3

Modeling with Polygons, Part 1

In both games and film, polygon modeling is a technique frequently used to build characters, sets, and props. Knowing how to model effectively with polygons is an important skill to have. In this chapter and the two that follow, you'll explore some poly modeling techniques.

▶ **Understanding polygons**

▶ **Constructing a good model**

▶ **Getting started and using the main modeling tools**

▶ **Box modeling and building a character**

Understanding Polygons

Polygons, or *polys*, are essentially flat surfaces that combine to make up a larger object. They're easy to work with and modify. Polygons, which are also called *faces*, are made up of smaller elements—vertices and edges.

Vertex

A *vertex* is a point in space. Each vertex (or *vert*) has X, Y, and Z coordinates for its location. Those coordinates are used by the Autodesk® Maya® software to track the object within the 3D environment. Any changes to the vert's position indicate some kind of movement, whether it's the whole object or just a component of it. Figure 3.1 shows a sphere with vertices visible.

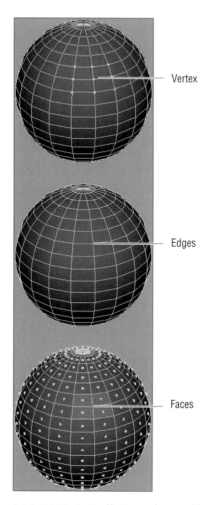

FIGURE 3.1 Vertices, edges, and faces

Edges

Edges are two vertices connected. Edges make up the borders of polygons. When modeling, you can extrude and modify edges to refine the shape of your model, as you'll see shortly. Three or more connected edges make a poly, or face. Figure 3.1 shows a sphere with edges selected and a sphere with faces selected.

Constructing a Good Model

There are some important factors to consider when building a model, especially one that will bend and deform like the character you're going to build. Good modeling technique means adhering to standard practices that lead to well-constructed models.

The Importance of Quads

Quads are polygons with four edges. Your goal is to *always* use quads in modeling. In a pinch, you can use a triangle, but quads are much more preferable. Quads render and deform well, and packages such as Pixologic's ZBrush and Autodesk® Mudbox® software require your model to be made of quads in order for you to work on them in the software. Figure 3.2 shows a quad poly.

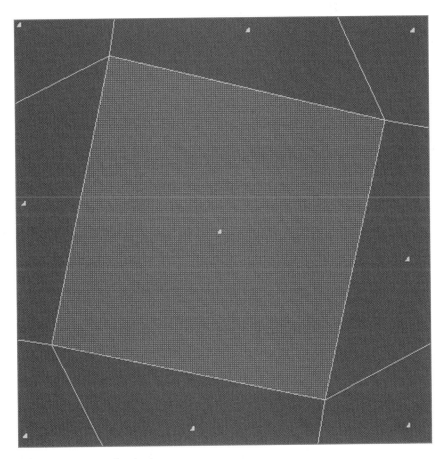

FIGURE 3.2   Quad polygon

The Problem With Ngons

Maya works best with quads and, to a lesser extent, triangles, or *tris*. But it is possible to make a polygon with more than four edges. These are referred to as *Ngons*. Except in very specific instances, you need to avoid having Ngons in your models. They can create many problems in deformation and rendering, and ZBrush and Mudbox won't import models with Ngons in them. It's surprisingly easy to create Ngons, so you have to constantly be on the lookout for them. Watch for any poly that has more than four edges around its perimeter. The easiest way to avoid Ngons is to be extremely careful when deleting edges; that's where many Ngons are created. Figure 3.3 shows an Ngon.

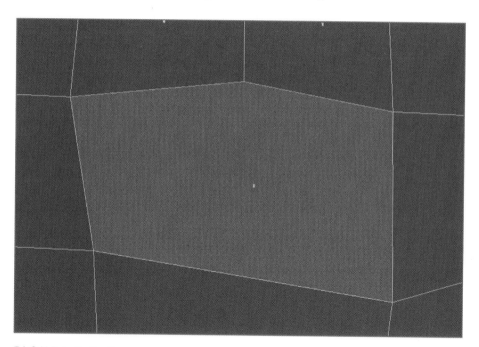

FIGURE 3.3 Ngon

Getting Started and Using the Main Modeling Tools

To get started modeling, you'll need to import some reference images, create a polygon primitive as a starting point, and work with a few tools to build your character.

Setting Up View Planes

To make modeling easier, you'll load reference images with front and side views. You can download the images used in the exercise at www.sybex.com/go/ maya2014essentials or use your own. The files provided are modelSketchFront .tif and modelSketchSide.tif. Create a new project as described in Chapter 2, "Creating Your First Animation." Call the project **characterModel**. Then follow these steps:

1. Place your reference images in the sourceimages folder.

2. Choose File ➢ New Scene.

3. Place your cursor in the scene window, and tap the spacebar to go to the four-panel view.

4. In the Front view, choose View ➢ Image Plane ➢ Import Image, as shown in Figure 3.4.

FIGURE 3.4   Importing the image

5. Navigate to your sourceimages folder, and select modelSketchFront.tif or your front-view sketch.

6. Repeat steps 4 and 5 in the Side view, and choose modelSketchSide.tif or your side-view sketch.

You now have front- and side-view sketches of the character you'll model in the scene, but the sketches are right in the middle of the environment. Next, you'll move them so they're still visible but won't get in the way when you start building your character:

1. In the Perspective view, click the edge of the `modelSketchFront` image. The edge highlights, as shown in Figure 3.5.

FIGURE 3.5   Front sketch selected

2. In the Channel Box, click imagePlaneShape1 under SHAPES.

3. Change the Image Center Z value to **-12**, as shown in Figure 3.6.

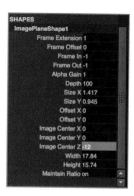

FIGURE 3.6   Changing the Image Center Z value for the front-view image plane

4. Again in the Perspective view, click the edge of the modelSketchSide image.

5. In the Channel Box, click imagePlaneShape2, and change the Image Center X value to -12, as shown in Figure 3.7.

FIGURE 3.7 Changing the Image Center X value for the side-view image plane

The reference images are now at the edges of the grid, as shown in Figure 3.8, but look the same in the Front and Side views as when they were in the center of the grid.

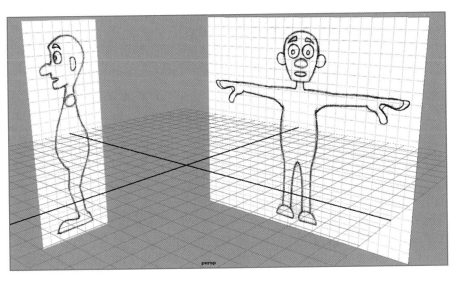

FIGURE 3.8 Reference images moved

Starting with a Cube

You're going to start your model with a polygon cube and use a technique called *box modeling* to build your character. Here are the steps:

1. Choose Create ➤ Polygon Primitives ➤ Cube ➤ Option Box.

2. In the Polygon Cube Options window, input the following values, as shown in Figure 3.9:

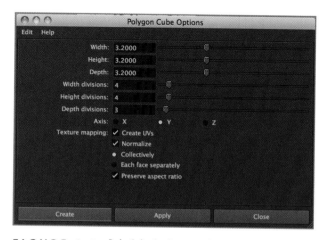

FIGURE 3.9   Poly Cube Options window

- ▶ Width, Height, Depth: 3.2
- ▶ Width Divisions and Height Divisions: 4
- ▶ Depth Divisions: 3

3. Click the Create button. A cube is created at the origin.

4. Place the cursor in each view, and press the 5 key to shade the cube.

5. Select the Move tool.

6. Click the cube (if it's not already selected), and move it up so it covers the head in the Front and Side views, as shown in Figure 3.10. Pan the view down so you can see the entire head in the sketch.

You're starting with a cube because it's the easiest shape to work with initially. It also requires the least geometry to create.

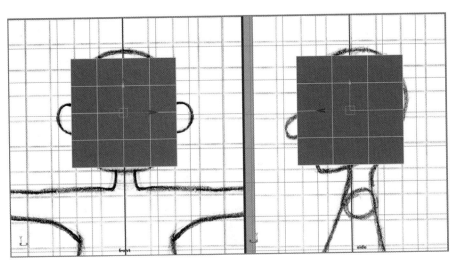

FIGURE 3.10   Cube moved

Extruding Faces

You'll rough in the basic form of your character by using the Extrude tool.
Then you'll add additional detail by using the Insert Edge Loop and Split
Polygon tools. Follow these steps:

1. Make sure the drop-down menu in the upper-left corner of the interface is set to Polygons. Then click the Edit Mesh menu and verify that
   Keep Faces Together is checked, as shown in Figure 3.11. If it's not,
   click it to check it.

Keep Faces Together
treats the selection as a
solid piece and inserts
faces only along the
selection perimeter.

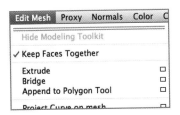

FIGURE 3.11   The Keep Faces Together option

2. Right-click the cube in any view to bring up the marking menu, and select Face.

3. Tumble the Perspective view so you can see the bottom of the cube. Select the center two faces on the bottom, as shown in Figure 3.12.

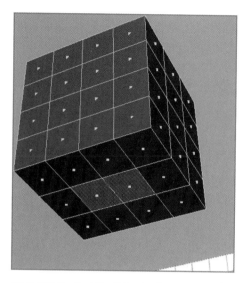

F I G U R E   3 . 1 2   Selecting faces to extrude

4. Switch to the Front view, and choose Edit Mesh ➢ Extrude, as shown in Figure 3.13.

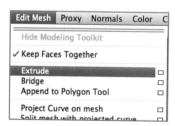

F I G U R E   3 . 1 3   Selecting the Extrude option

5. Click the blue (Z axis) arrowhead, and drag down. New faces appear. Drag until the bottom edge of the new faces is the length of the neck in the sketch, as shown in Figure 3.14.

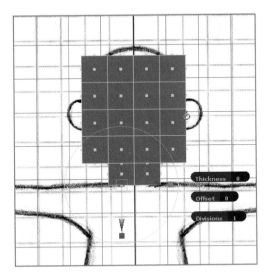

FIGURE 3.14 Moving extruded faces

Box Modeling and Building a Character

Now that you've extruded some faces from your cube, you'll extrude out the main shapes of the character. After you have those in, you'll go back and add detail with the Insert Edge Loop and Split Polygon tools. Follow these steps:

1. With the bottom faces still selected, choose Edit Mesh ➢ Extrude again, or press g on your keyboard. The g key repeats the last command you performed.

2. Click the blue arrowhead, and drag down to create a shoulder area.

3. Click the red cube (X scale), and drag to the right to scale the new faces to the width of the torso, as shown in Figure 3.15.

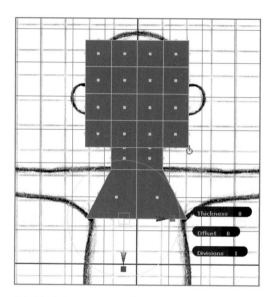

FIGURE 3.15   Scaling faces

4. Press g to extrude another set of faces, and then drag them down the length of the torso. Select the X scale handle, and scale the faces so they're the width of the bottom of the torso, as shown in Figure 3.16.

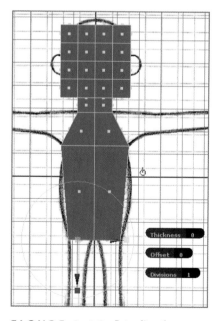

FIGURE 3.16   Extruding the torso

5. Switch to the Perspective view. Select the face on the bottom of the torso, at the right side of the screen, as shown in Figure 3.17.

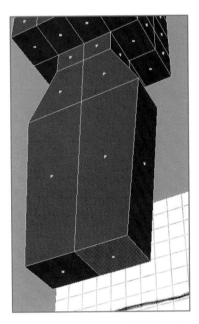

FIGURE 3.17 Single-face selection

6. Return to the Front view, and extrude a set of polys for the leg, as shown in Figure 3.18. Scale on the X axis, and move right on the X slightly.

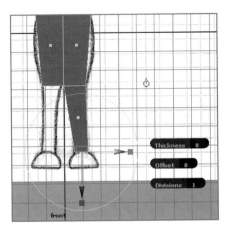

FIGURE 3.18 Leg extrusion

7. Extrude one more time to create the foot height, as shown in Figure 3.19.

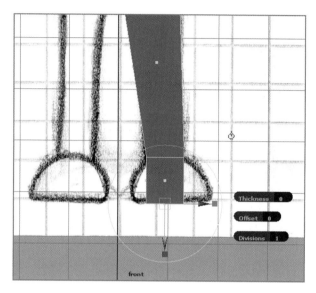

FIGURE 3.19 Foot extrusion

8. Select the front face of the preceding extrusion, as shown in Figure 3.20.

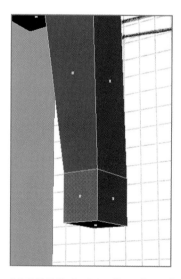

FIGURE 3.20 Front face selection

9. Switch to the Side view and extrude, moving the new faces on the Z axis, as shown in Figure 3.21.

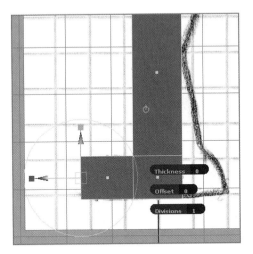

FIGURE 3.21 Second foot extrusion

10. Switch to the Perspective view. Select the face on the side, just below the neck, as shown in Figure 3.22.

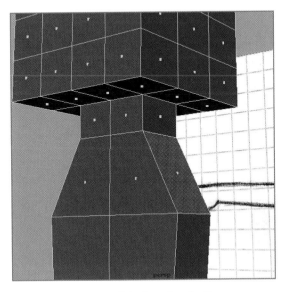

FIGURE 3.22 Selecting a face for the arm

11. Switch to the Front view. Choose Edit Mesh ➢ Extrude.

12. Click the small circle icon above and to the right of the manipulator handle, as shown in Figure 3.23. The manipulator handles switch orientation.

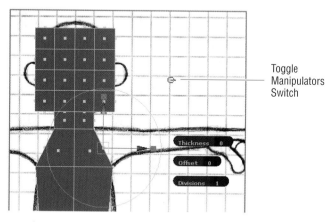

Toggle
Manipulators
Switch

FIGURE 3.23 Manipulators' toggle switch

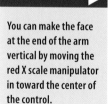

You can make the face at the end of the arm vertical by moving the red X scale manipulator in toward the center of the control.

13. Drag out the new faces. Scale and move the selected face so that it looks like Figure 3.24.

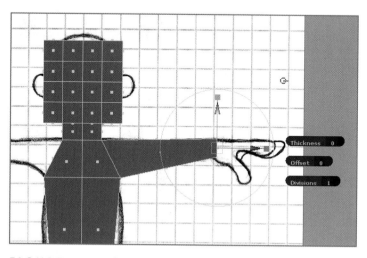

FIGURE 3.24 Extruding the arm

14. Extrude the face again to create the palm base, as shown in Figure 3.25.

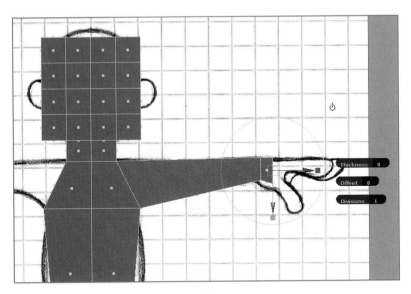

FIGURE 3.25   Extruding the palm base

15. Extrude once more to create the rest of the palm, as shown in Figure 3.26.

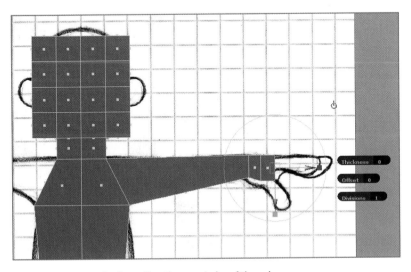

FIGURE 3.26   Extruding the remainder of the palm

16. Select the faces on the front and back of the most recent extrusion, and extrude again, as shown in Figure 3.27.

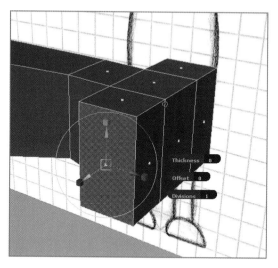

FIGURE 3.27   Building the finger base

17. Select the three faces on the end of the arm, and extrude them again to create the finger base, as shown in Figure 3.28.

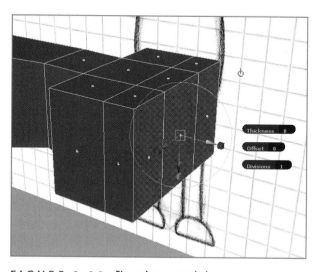

FIGURE 3.28   Finger base extruded

18. Select the center of the three end faces, press R to activate the Scale tool, and scale in on the Z axis until the three end faces are about the same size, as shown in Figure 3.29.

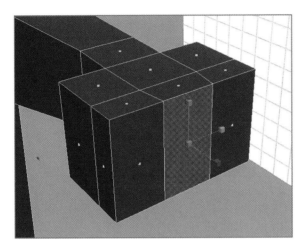

FIGURE 3.29   Scaling the finger base

19. Choose Edit Mesh ➢ Keep Faces Together to turn off the Keep Faces Together option.

20. Select the three end polys on the finger base.

21. Choose Edit Mesh ➢ Extrude, and move the faces out on the Z axis.

22. Click any of the scale manipulator boxes to activate the Scale function, and then scale using the center of the manipulator to taper the finger sections slightly, as shown in Figure 3.30.

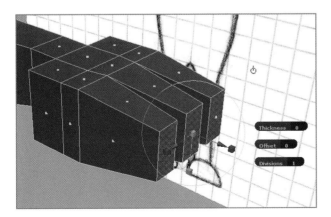

FIGURE 3.30   Finger extrusion

23. Choose Edit Mesh ➤ Keep Faces Together to turn the Keep Faces Together option back on.

24. To create a thumb, select the poly on the side of section of the palm with three divisions, as shown in Figure 3.31.

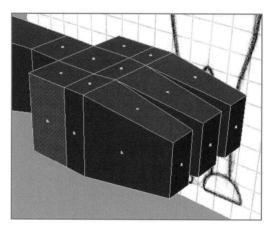

FIGURE 3.31　Selecting the thumb base

25. Choose Edit Mesh ➤ Extrude, and click a scale handle to activate the Scale function.

26. Scale the selected poly by using the center handle, as shown in Figure 3.32.

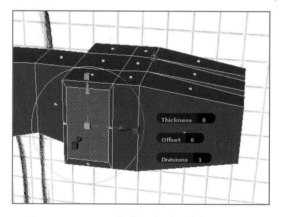

FIGURE 3.32　Scaling the thumb base

27. Extrude again, and pull the poly out on the Z axis, as shown in Figure 3.33. In the figure, the thumb has also been tapered slightly as the fingers were.

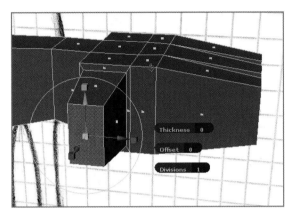

FIGURE 3.33 Extruding the thumb

You've now blocked in the main shapes of your character. Now it's time to refine and add some details.

Refining the Character's Geometry

You're probably wondering why you created only one arm and leg. It's easier and faster to model one half of a symmetrical object such as a character. Then, when you have finished half, you'll reflect that geometry over the center axis to complete the model. Here are the steps:

1. Right-click on the model, and select Face from the marking menu.

2. In the Front view, select all the faces on the screen-left side of the character (the side without the leg and arm).

3. Press the Delete key. The selected faces are deleted, as shown in Figure 3.34.

One of the primary rules of modeling is to keep your geometry as simple as possible for as long as possible. This makes it easier to refine the shapes without a lot of extra faces and verts to deal with. You can always add more detail later, as you'll do in this chapter.

FIGURE 3.34   Faces deleted

4. Right-click on the model again to bring up the marking menu, and select Object Mode. The model is now selected as an object and ready for refining.

Using the Insert Edge Loop Tool

You'll start to refine your model by using the Insert Edge Loop tool to add additional geometry. This tool inserts edges at points you specify, effectively splitting existing polygons in two. The Insert Edge Loop tool works only on quad polys. Follow these steps:

1. Choose Edit Mesh ➤ Insert Edge Loop Tool.

2. Click and hold the vertical edge in the middle of the character's torso. A dotted line appears, as shown in Figure 3.35.

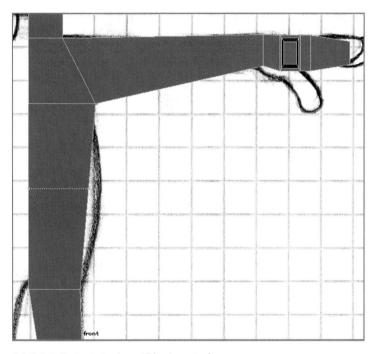

FIGURE 3.35   Insert Edge Loop tool

3. Drag the dotted line to a point in the torso where you'd like to make adjustments to the shape. Then release the mouse button. A new edge is inserted, as shown in Figure 3.36.

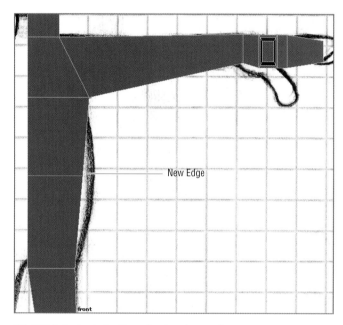

FIGURE 3.36   New edge loop inserted

4. Using the Insert Edge Loop tool, insert new edges at the elbow and knee, as shown in Figure 3.37.

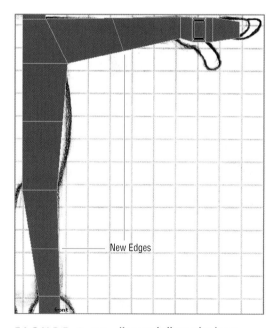

FIGURE 3.37   Knee and elbow edge loops

5. Insert an edge loop running through the arm, hand, fingers, and torso, as shown in Figure 3.38.

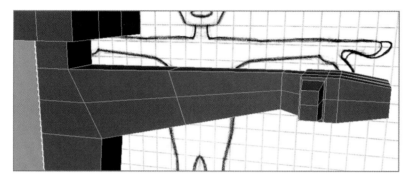

FIGURE 3.38 Arm edge loop

6. Insert an edge loop that runs up the front of the foot, leg, torso, neck, and head, as shown in Figure 3.39.

FIGURE 3.39 Leg edge loop

Using the Split Polygon Tool

When you added the leg loop, it went all the way around the model and added geometry to the face that you really don't need. You're going to use the Split Polygon tool to terminate that loop under the character's chin while maintaining the quad polys you're working with:

1. Press Q to exit the Insert Edge Loop tool.

2. Right-click on the model, and select Edge from the marking menu.

3. In the Perspective view, select the edge under the head block, as shown in Figure 3.40.

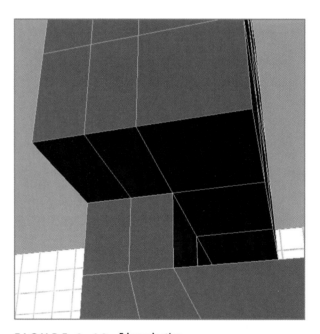

FIGURE 3.40   Edge selection

4. Delete the edge by choosing Edit Mesh ➢ Delete Edge/Vertex.

5. Right-click on your model, and select Object Mode.

Using Delete Edge/ Vertex ensures that any leftover verts are deleted along with the edge. This helps prevent accidental ngon creation.

6. Click the model to select it, and then hold down Shift and right-click on the model. Drag to Split; then, when the menu changes, drag to Split Polygon tool, as shown in Figure 3.41.

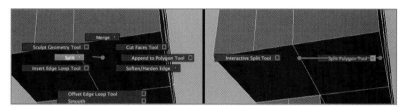

FIGURE 3.41 Split Polygon tool menu

7. In the Tool Settings window, uncheck the Split Only From Edges check box. Set Snapping Tolerance to **25**, as shown in Figure 3.42.

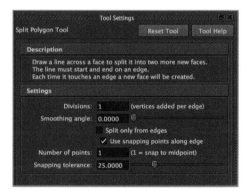

FIGURE 3.42 Split Polygon tool settings

8. Click and drag the bottom edge of the cube to set the first point, making sure the point is on the vertex where the edges meet. (Be sure your new point is at the intersection of the two edges to keep from creating ngons.) Then click in the center of the face to set the second point. Finally, click and drag the edge where the neck shape meets the head, as shown in Figure 3.43. If any of the points end up where they shouldn't be, press Delete and reset the point.

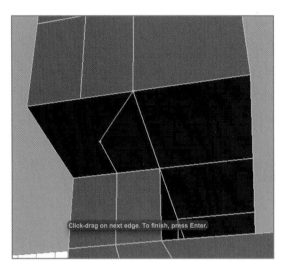

FIGURE 3.43   Setting edge points

9. Press Return/Enter to create the edge, as shown in Figure 3.44.

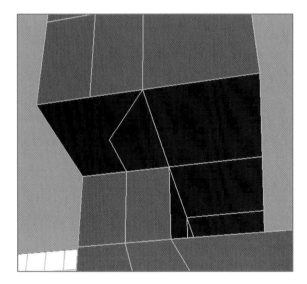

FIGURE 3.44   Edge created

10. Press y to reselect the Split Polygon tool.

11. Set a point at the corner of the new edge and a second point on the edge to the left.

12. Press Return/Enter to create the edge, as shown in Figure 3.45.

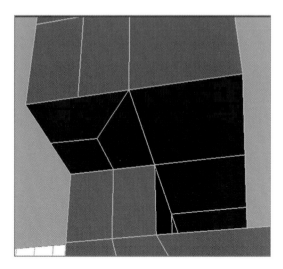

FIGURE 3.45 Second edge created

13. Repeat steps 1–12 on the other side of the head shape. The result is shown in Figure 3.46.

FIGURE 3.46 Second split complete

14. Return to the front of the model, and in edge selection mode, double-click the edge shown in Figure 3.47.

FIGURE 3.47   Edge selected

15. Choose Edit Mesh ➢ Delete Edge/Vertex to delete the selected edges. The result is shown in Figure 3.48.

FIGURE 3.48   Extra edges deleted

Shaping Your Character

Now that you have the basic geometry in place, you can begin sculpting it to make it look more like the sketches on the image planes. Follow these steps:

1. In the Front and Side views, choose Shading ➤ X-Ray, as shown in Figure 3.49.

FIGURE 3.49   X-Ray shading

2. Right-click on the model in either view to bring up the marking menu, and select Vertex.

3. Using the Move, Rotate, and Scale tools and working in the Front and Side views, move the vertices on the model to more closely match the contour of the sketches, as shown in Figure 3.50.

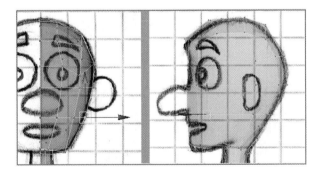

FIGURE 3.50   Vertex adjustment

Someone once said that when you're modeling, you'll touch every vert on the model, sometimes more than once. This is very true. Just take your time, refer to your sketches often, and keep in mind that the goal is a nice, rounded (not boxy) model.

4. Continue moving vertices around to make your character look more like the sketches. Keep in mind that the shapes of the body should be rounded looking, not square. After a lot of vertex moving, your model

should look similar to Figure 3.51. To see what your model will look like when it's smoothed, press 3 on your keyboard to create a smooth proxy. You can reposition vertices with the smooth proxy on, but take care not to move any vertex too far. Check your low-poly model frequently by pressing 1 to return to poly view mode. In Figure 3.51, another edge loop has been added between the top of the leg and the lower torso loop to provide more control over the torso shape.

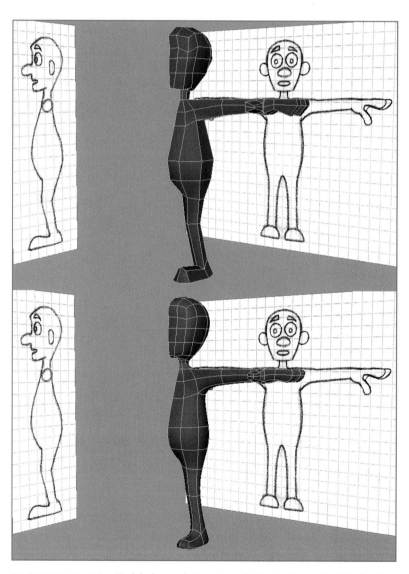

F I G U R E 3 . 5 1   Model after sculpting: low poly (top) and smoothed (bottom)

THE ESSENTIALS AND BEYOND

In this chapter, you modeled the main shapes for your character by using the Extrude, Insert Edge Loop, and Split Polygon tools, along with moving vertices. This is the starting point for all modeling done in Maya. When you're creating a model, it's important to keep the geometry as light as possible, adding only as much as is absolutely necessary to create the shapes you need. In the next chapter, you'll add details to the head.

Additional Exercises

▶ Model a prop for your character to use. Keep it simple, and use the techniques you learned in creating your character model.

▶ Add some additional edge loops to parts of the character that will bend. Fingers, the foot, and the torso are good candidates.

CHAPTER 4

Modeling with Polygons, Part 2

An important consideration when modeling is how your polygons are organized and arranged. Your character will be animated using a couple of kinds of deformations, so you have to create poly arrangements that will deform well without causing surface problems. In this chapter, you'll tackle the facial details, including creating edge loops around facial elements so they'll deform well.

▶ **Creating edge loops**

▶ **Adjusting vertices, polygons, and edges, and adding details**

Creating Edge Loops

Edge loops are rings of edges that mimic the layout of muscles, in this case in the face. When modeling, you want to create edge loops so that parts such as mouth shapes and eyelids will work properly when you create facial expressions. The finished edge loops you'll create in this chapter are shown in Figure 4.1.

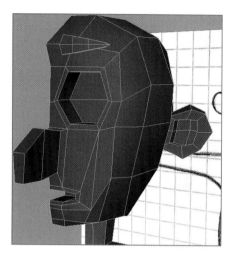

FIGURE 4.1   Facial edge loops

Getting Started: Deleting Edges and Setting Tool Options

Your first steps in creating facial details are to delete some edges you won't need and set up the Split Polygon tool, which you'll use to create your edge loops:

1. Start with your model from Chapter 3, "Modeling with Polygons, Part 1," or open Ch4Start.ma. If you're using Ch4Start.ma, save the file to the scenes folder in your project directory.

2. Zoom in on the front of the head, as shown in Figure 4.2. Select Shading ➢ Wireframe on Shaded in the View menu.

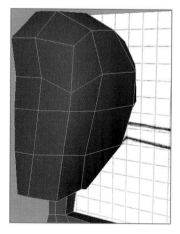

FIGURE 4.2   Your starting point on the face

3. Right-click on the model to bring up the marking menu, and select Edge.

4. Select the three edges shown in Figure 4.3.

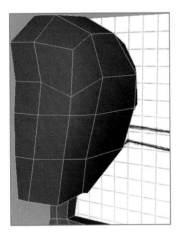

FIGURE 4.3 Edge selection

5. From the Polygons menu set, choose Edit Mesh ➢ Delete Edge/Vertex, as shown in Figure 4.4.

FIGURE 4.4 Choosing the Delete Edge/Vertex option

6. Deleting the edges has created an Ngon that you'll break up by using the Split Polygon tool. Right-click on the model, and select Object Mode. Click on the object to select it, hold down Shift and right-click, and drag to Split and then Split Polygon Tool, as shown in Figure 4.5.

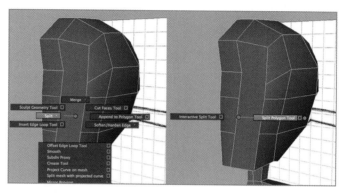

FIGURE 4.5   Choosing Split Polygon Tool from the Hotbox

7. Verify that Split only from edges is unchecked in the Tool Settings window, as shown in Figure 4.6. Click on the X button to close the window.

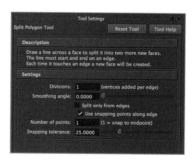

FIGURE 4.6   Split Polygon Tool Settings window

Building Your Edge Loops

Now that you have your tool set correctly, it's time to start creating edge loops for the face:

1. Using the Split Polygon tool, lay out the edges shown in Figure 4.7.

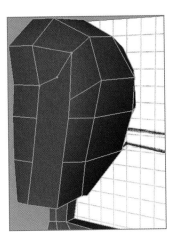

FIGURE 4.7   The first edges
of the edge loop

2. Press Return/Enter to create the new edges.

3. Press y to reactivate the Split Polygon tool, and create another new poly, as shown in Figure 4.8.

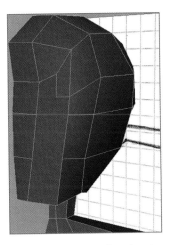

FIGURE 4.8   Creating the
second poly

When you're placing points on existing edges, make sure you're putting those points directly on top of the existing vertices. If you miss, you're creating Ngons. Existing vertices are located anywhere that two edges connect. A good way to make sure you're placing points on top of existing vertices is to click and hold a short distance away from a corner and then drag to the corner, stopping when the point stops moving.

4. Repeat step 3 twice to create two more polys, one at a time, as shown in Figure 4.9.

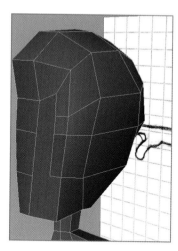

FIGURE 4.9   Creating two more polys

Occasionally, the Split Polygon tool will place the point you set on the opposite side of the polygon you're working on. When this happens, you'll click to set a point and see no visual confirmation that the point was created. If this happens, you can switch temporarily to x-ray mode (Shading ➢ X-ray) to see the points being set.

5. Create another poly, as shown in Figure 4.10.

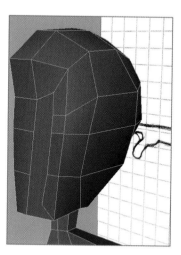

FIGURE 4.10   Creating the bottom-corner poly

6. Continuing to use the Split Polygon tool, create a new split as shown in Figure 4.11.

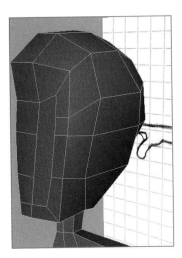

FIGURE 4.11 Creating the initial split

7. Create three final splits that connect the edges on the Ngon all the way to the center of the character, as shown in Figure 4.12.

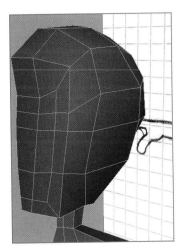

FIGURE 4.12 Creating the final three splits

8. To start the mouth loop, use the Split Polygon tool to create an edge, as shown in Figure 4.13.

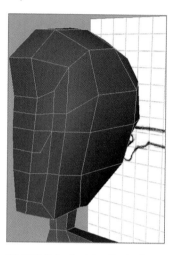

FIGURE 4.13 Beginning the mouth loop

9. Create a quad poly for the outside of the mouth loop, as shown in Figure 4.14.

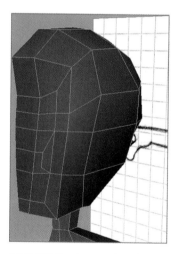

FIGURE 4.14 Completing the loop for the corner of the mouth

10. Finish the mouth loop by extending it to the center edge, as shown in Figure 4.15.

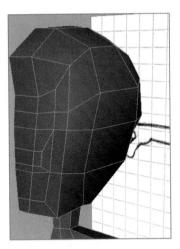

FIGURE 4.15   Mouth loop completed

11. Select Edit Mesh ➢ Insert Edge Loop Tool, and create another edge loop around the mouth loop you just created, as shown in Figure 4.16. To insert the loop, click on the vertical edge right above the mouth loop you just created. This loop will allow you to shape the lips later.

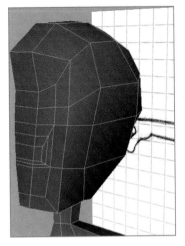

FIGURE 4.16   Creating the outer mouth loop

12. Press q to exit the Insert Edge Loop tool. Using the marking menu, switch to Face selection mode, select the two faces in the middle of the mouth loop, and extrude them inward, as shown in Figure 4.17. If your manipulator is at an angle, click on the Toggle Manipulators Switch as you did in Chapter 3 and extrude the new faces straight back.

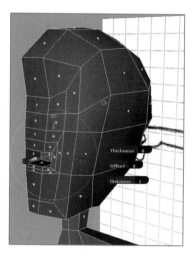

FIGURE 4.17   Extruding the interior of the mouth

13. Select the two faces where the eye socket will be, and select Extrude. Select scale mode, and scale using the center manipulator, creating a new edge loop around the eye socket, as shown in Figure 4.18.

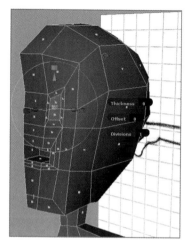

FIGURE 4.18   Extruding the eye loop

14. Extrude the selected faces again, and move them inward to create the eye socket, as shown in Figure 4.19.

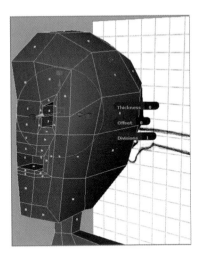

FIGURE 4.19 Extruding the eye socket

15. Tumble the view so you can see into the model from the left side of the character, as shown in Figure 4.20. Select the face shown in the figure, and press Delete. This face has to be deleted so that when you mirror the character, the mouth is open without a face down the center.

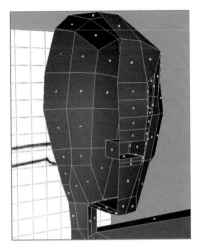

FIGURE 4.20 Selecting the center face of the mouth

Adjusting Vertices, Polygons, and Edges, and Adding Details

With all your edge loops are in place, you can begin sculpting your character to create the facial features. You'll move existing verts and extrude new geometry to build the features.

1. Switch to the Front view, turn on Shading/X-Ray as you did in the preceding chapter, and choose Display ≻ Polygons ≻ Custom Polygon Display. The Custom Polygon Display Options window opens, as shown in Figure 4.21. Scroll to the bottom of the window, and turn on Backface Culling. This setting hides the back faces of the model, allowing you to work on just the vertices on the front of the model.

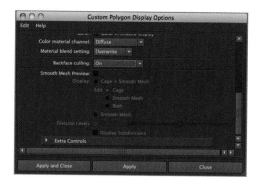

FIGURE 4.21   Turning on Backface Culling

2. Move vertices around so the geometry of the character matches the sketch on the view plane. When you're finished, your model should look something like Figure 4.22.

3. Select the face at the center edge between the eye loop and the mouth loop.

4. Extrude the face and scale inward so the face looks similar to Figure 4.23. This creates the base of the nose.

It's a good idea to drag-select the vertices you want to move. In many cases, multiple verts line up, and drag-selecting is a good way to get them all at once.

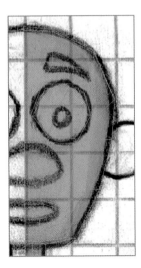

FIGURE 4.22 Moving
vertices to match the sketch

Figure 4.23 has x-ray shading turned off for clarity. You can work
with it either on or off, as you prefer.

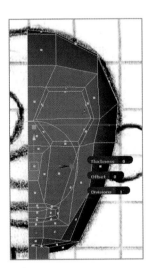

FIGURE 4.23 Extruding
the base of the nose

5. Switch to the Side view, and extrude two more times. Scale each extrusion to roughly follow the sketch on the view plane. When you're finished, your model should look similar to Figure 4.24.

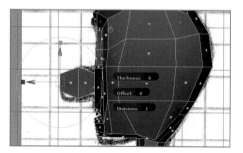

FIGURE 4.24   Extruding the nose

6. Using the marking menu, switch to vertex mode and reposition the vertices on the nose shape to more closely match the sketch. Your finished nose will look similar to Figure 4.25.

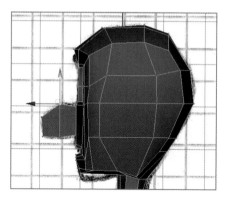

FIGURE 4.25   Adjusting the nose verts

7. Tumble the Perspective view so you can see the inside edge of the nose, and delete the three faces running down the middle of the nose shape, as shown in Figure 4.26.

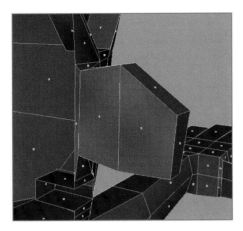

FIGURE 4.26   Extra nose faces to be deleted

8. In the Side view, with XRay turned on, select the two faces nearest the location of the ear in the sketch. If you need to move verts a bit to make the faces align with the ear, feel free. The selected faces are shown in Figure 4.27.

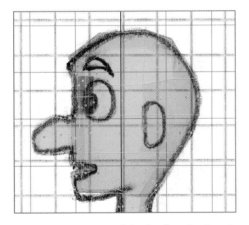

FIGURE 4.27   Selecting faces for the ear

9. Just as you did with the nose, extrude a new set of faces, and scale them inward to create the ear base, as shown in Figure 4.28.

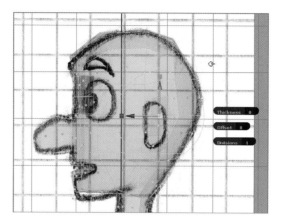

FIGURE 4.28 Extruding and scaling a poly for the ear base

10. Switch to the Front view, and extrude again. Click on the Toggle Manipulators Switch, if necessary, and pull out the new faces to create a rough ear shape, as shown in Figure 4.29.

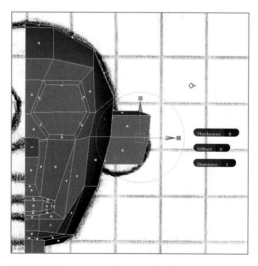

FIGURE 4.29 Ear extruded

11. Use the Insert Edge Loop tool to create a vertical edge loop similar to the one in Figure 4.30. Move the ear verts around to create an ear shape similar to the sketch.

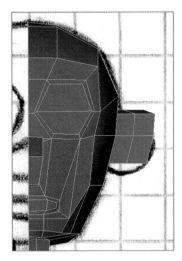

FIGURE 4.30 Ear edge loop inserted

12. Switch to Perspective view, and select the four faces in the center of the front of the ear. Extrude, and scale inward, as shown in Figure 4.31.

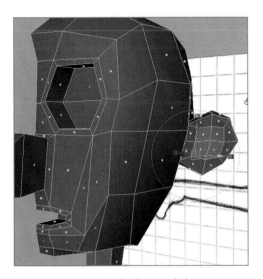

FIGURE 4.31 Ear faces scaled

13. Extrude one more time, scale the faces slightly inward, and move them toward the back of the ear, taking care not to move them through the other ear faces. Figure 4.32 shows what this looks like.

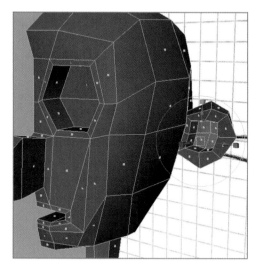

FIGURE 4.32   Final ear faces positioned

Creating Eyebrows

Finally, you'll create a new piece of geometry for the eyebrow, combining it with the main model so Maya treats it all as one piece:

1. Create a polygon cube with the values shown in Figure 4.33.

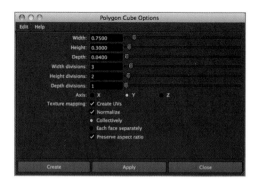

FIGURE 4.33   Polygon cube values

2. The cube appears near the middle of your character. Move it up to the eyebrow position, and move verts around until you get a shape similar to Figure 4.34. Be sure to move the box to the front of the head geometry.

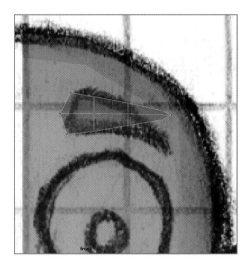

FIGURE 4.34   Eyebrow geometry sculpted

3. In Object Mode, select the eyebrow, and then Shift-select the main model. Select Mesh ➤ Combine, as shown in Figure 4.35. This command tells Maya that all the selected geometry is to be treated as a single piece.

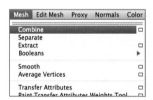

FIGURE 4.35   Mesh a Combine menu item

The brow is modeled in a more neutral position than in the sketch. This is to provide more flexibility when creating blend shapes for the eyebrow. The brow is also bent slightly to curve around the contour of the character's head. These are classic cartoony "floating" eyebrows, which are easier to create and much more fun to work with!

You may notice that the model looks a bit different than the sketch in places. Sometimes it's necessary to alter design elements in order to make them work in 3D. Anything's possible in a 2D sketch; in 3D, the shapes have to work on every axis. Remember to toggle between polygon view and the smooth proxy to check your work (1 and 3 are the keys that toggle the view).

4. Switch to the Perspective view and tumble the view, looking at your character's face in both polygon and smooth mode, as shown in Figure 4.36. Make any final tweaks you feel are necessary to get the look you want.

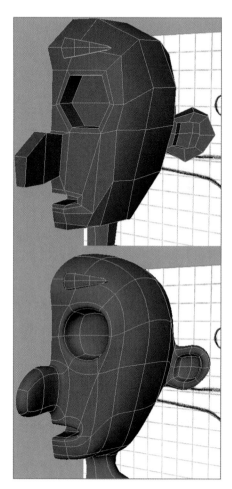

FIGURE 4.36 Character's face (poly view and smoothed)

THE ESSENTIALS AND BEYOND

Creating edge loops around features such as the eyes and the mouth is essential to ensuring proper deformation when you animate those shapes. You've also spent some time repositioning vertices and faces to get elements of your model to match the design sketches as closely as possible.

ADDITIONAL EXERCISES

▶ Turn on the Poly Count Heads-Up Display (Display ➤ Heads Up Display ➤ Poly Count), and, in vertex mode, select some of the intersections where you started new edges. On the Verts line of the Heads-Up Display (HUD), check the third column to see how many verts are selected. Note the ones where the number is higher than 1—you'll fix those in the next chapter.

▶ Add any additional features you'd like your character to have, using the eyebrow addition method. Mustaches, ties, buttons, and many other details can be added using this technique.

CHAPTER 5

Modeling with Polygons, Part 3

Now that your character model is in pretty good shape and has facial geometry that will deform well, it's time for the last few steps that will prepare the character for rigging and animation. You'll add some geometry to ensure that your character deforms well once the skeleton is added, mirror the existing geometry to complete the character, and delete the modeling history.

▶ **Refining and cleaning up**

▶ **Mirroring your model**

▶ **Deleting history**

Refining and Cleaning Up

You need to take some final steps to finish your character and get it set for rigging. These procedures will make sure your character moves as well as possible, eliminate any extraneous geometry, positions the character well for rigging, and, of course, create the other half of the character.

Adding Geometry for Good Deformations

Before you complete the character by mirroring the existing half, you want to be sure all the areas where bending will occur (elbows, knees, and so forth) have enough geometry to support the bending. If there isn't enough geometry, the model will collapse in on itself. Here are the steps:

1. Open your model from the preceding chapter, or use
   Chapter5Start.ma.

2. Select the Insert Edge Loop tool, and add edge loops to the elbow area. You should have a total of three loops, as shown in Figure 5.1.

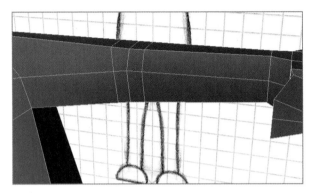

FIGURE 5.1   Elbow edge loops

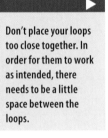

Don't place your loops too close together. In order for them to work as intended, there needs to be a little space between the loops.

3. Add two more edge loops to the shoulder area, as shown in Figure 5.2.

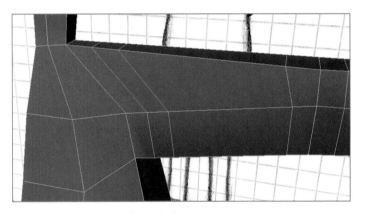

FIGURE 5.2   Shoulder edge loops

4. Add two more edge loops to the wrist area, as shown in Figure 5.3.

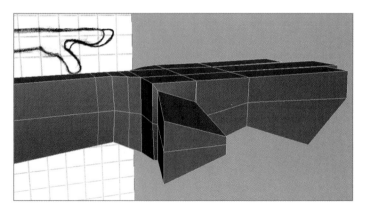

FIGURE 5.3 Wrist edge loops

5. Add edge loops to the hip, knee, ankle, and toe, as shown in Figure 5.4.

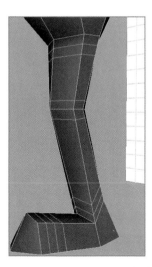

FIGURE 5.4 Leg edge loops

6. Add an edge loop to the base of the foot to help flatten out the bottom, as shown in Figure 5.5. The closer together edge loops are arranged, the sharper the transition between them. The two loops close together provide a flatter bottom surface for the foot.

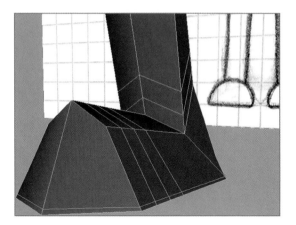

FIGURE 5.5   Foot base edge loop

7. Add edge loops to the neck and fingers, as shown in Figure 5.6.

FIGURE 5.6   Neck and finger edge loops

8. Make sure you have a few edge loops in the torso, as shown in Figure 5.7.

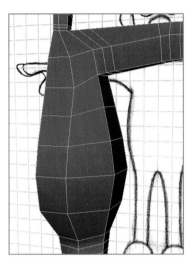

FIGURE 5.7   Torso edge loops

9. Make any final changes to the geometry that you'd like. In the smoothed proxy in Figure 5.8, the nose, arm, fingers, leg, foot, and inside of the mouth have been resculpted to more closely match the sketch. Also, another edge loop has been added around the lips to create a sharper transition from the outside to the inside of the mouth.

FIGURE 5.8   Final modeling adjustments

Cleaning Up the Model

While you're modeling, it's easy for stray vertices to find their way into your model if you either delete edges without using Delete Edge/Vertex or accidentally click the mouse while using the Split Polygon tool. These extra verts can cause problems when you rig your model for animation. To get rid of any extra verts that may be in the model, you're going to do a merge operation:

1. Right-click on the model, and select Vertex mode.

2. Drag-select over the entire model to select all the vertices, as shown in Figure 5.9.

FIGURE 5.9 Model vertices selected

3. Choose Edit Mesh ➢ Merge ➢ option box, as shown in Figure 5.10.

4. The Merge Vertices Options window opens. Set the Threshold value to a very low number, such as **0.0010**, as shown in Figure 5.11. Click on the Merge button.

FIGURE 5.10 Edit
Mesh a Merge a option box
menu choice

FIGURE 5.11 Merge Vertices Options window

5. Inspect your model carefully to make sure no verts intended to be
on the surface of the model were accidentally merged. The geometry
of the model should look unchanged from what you built. If verts
were merged, press z to undo, and repeat steps 3 and 4 with a lower
Threshold value.

The Threshold number
is set low so verts that
are very close together
will merge, while leav-
ing verts that are far-
ther apart as they are.

Positioning Your Character for Rigging

Although it doesn't technically matter where your model is when you rig it, it's good modeling practice to have your character's feet on the grid. Follow these steps to position your character:

1. Switch to the Front view.

2. In the view window, select the Show menu, and turn the Grid option back on. Figure 5.12 shows the location of the Grid option.

FIGURE 5.12
Show a Grid option

3. Select your model in Object Mode.

4. Press w to activate the Move tool.

5. The manipulator handle should be in the center of your character. If it is, skip to step 8. If it's not, press and hold the d key. The Move Pivot tool appears, as shown in Figure 5.13.

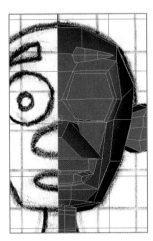

FIGURE 5.13 Move Pivot tool

6. Click the vertical handle, and drag so the Move Pivot tool is in the middle of your character, as shown in Figure 5.14.

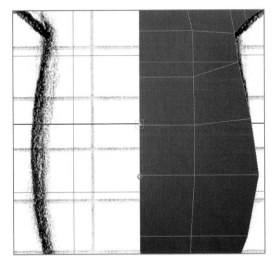

FIGURE 5.14 Pivot tool moved

7. Release the d key to deactivate the Move Pivot tool.

8. Click the Y move handle (the green arrowhead), and move your model up so the feet are resting on the horizontal black line, as shown in Figure 5.15.

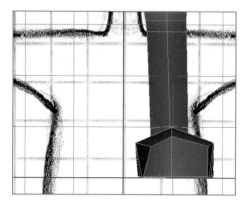

FIGURE 5.15   Model moved

9. Choose Modify ➢ Freeze Transformations, as shown in Figure 5.16. This operation zeroes out the Move and Rotate values, making it easy to reposition your model if necessary.

FIGURE 5.16
Freeze transformations

Adding Eyeballs

One last modeling task to tackle is to add eyeballs to your character. Because they move independent of the body, eyeballs are nearly always created as separate objects, which are then parented to the skeletal structure during rigging so that they move when the head moves. To create an eyeball for your character, perform the following steps:

1. Switch to the Front view, and zoom in on the model's eye socket. Press 3 to switch to smooth proxy mode.

2. Turn on XRay mode by clicking on the button shown in Figure 5.17.

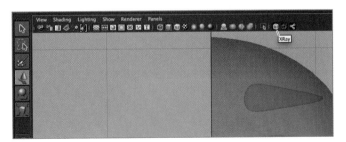

FIGURE 5.17 XRay mode button

3. Go to Create ➢ Polygon Primitives, and turn on Interactive Creation.

4. Select Create ➢ Polygon Primitives ➢ Sphere, as seen in Figure 5.18.

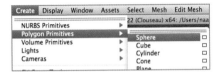

FIGURE 5.18 Create Polygon Sphere
menu choice

5. Place your cursor in the center of the eye socket, and drag out a sphere roughly the size of the socket, as shown in Figure 5.19.

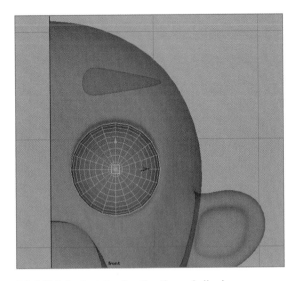

FIGURE 5.19 Creating the eyeball sphere

6. Switch to the Perspective view, and move the eyeball into position in the eye socket. Make any adjustments to the eye-socket vertices so that the socket conforms to the surface of the eyeball, as Figure 5.20 shows. You want the eye socket to just touch the surface of the eyeball, not pass through it.

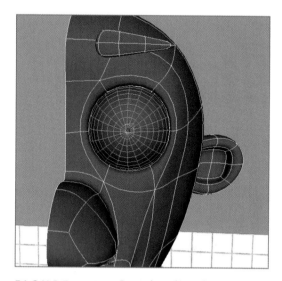

FIGURE 5.20 Eye socket adjusted

Mirroring Your Model

With your model in place, you will finish it by mirroring the existing geometry and attaching the copied geometry to the existing model. First, you'll make sure all the vertices along the center of your model are aligned with the 0 (zero) point on the X axis. To do this, you're going to use a short Maya Embedded Language (MEL) script:

1. Right-click on the main model, and select Vertex mode.

2. In the Front view, drag-select all the vertices along the centerline of your character, as shown in Figure 5.21.

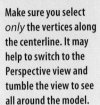

Make sure you select *only* the vertices along the centerline. It may help to switch to the Perspective view and tumble the view to see all around the model.

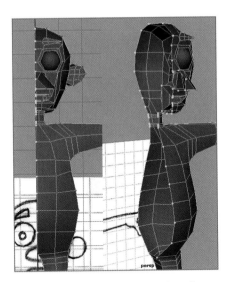

FIGURE 5.21 Vertices selected

3. Locate the MEL window below the Range Slider, as shown in Figure 5.22.

FIGURE 5.22 MEL window

If *Python* appears next to the MEL window, click the word to switch to MEL.

4. Type the following text into the MEL window:

```
move -a -x 0;
```

5. Press Return/Enter.

6. Choose Mesh ➤ Mirror Geometry ➤ option box, as shown in Figure 5.23. The Mirror Options window opens, as shown in Figure 5.24.

This MEL command moves all the selected vertices to the 0 point on the X axis This guarantees that all the vertices are aligned at 0 X while keeping their positions on both the Y and Z axes.

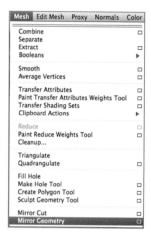

FIGURE 5.23 Mirror Geometry option

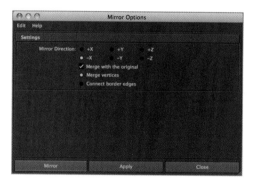

FIGURE 5.24 Mirror Options window

7. Set Mirror Direction to -X. Make sure the options Merge With The Original and Merge Vertices are selected, and then click Mirror. The model's geometry is reflected across the Y axis and connected to the existing geometry, completing the model as shown in Figure 5.25.

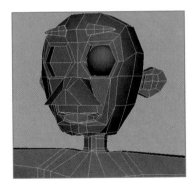

FIGURE 5.25 Model mirrored

Notice in Figure 5.25 that some of the verts in the neck and mouth area have been inadvertently merged into each other. This is because the Mirror function has a preset merge threshold. Any verts closer together than the merge threshold are automatically merged during the mirror operation. Fortunately, this is easy to fix:

1. In the Channel Box, under Inputs, click on polyMirror1 to open the node.

2. Click on the Merge Threshold value, and lower it to a very small number like 0.01, as shown in Figure 5.26. Press Enter/Return. The merged verts should separate and give you a result similar to the one shown in Figure 5.27. If not, try a lower value until they do.

FIGURE 5.26
Merge Threshold value

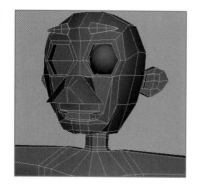

FIGURE 5.27   Corrected verts

Occasionally, the mirror function doesn't mirror correctly, leaving a gap between the halves of the character or overlapping the halves. If that happens, undo the mirror and complete the "Deleting History" procedure that follows, and then try mirroring again. Deleting the modeling history will often cause the mirror operation to complete successfully.

Deleting History

To prepare your model for rigging, you must delete the modeling history. If the modeling history is retained, it can occasionally conflict with the deformers used to animate the character, creating problems that can be tricky to solve. Deleting modeling history removes one potential problem, making the task of troubleshooting easier.

1. Select the model in object mode.

2. Look at the Channel Box, as shown in Figure 5.28. Every modeling action you've performed is listed under INPUTS. Scroll down through the list to see how much was done to create your model.

FIGURE 5.28
Channel Box inputs

3. Choose Edit ➢ Delete By Type ➢ History, as shown in Figure 5.29.

FIGURE 5.29   Delete By Type a History

4. Check the Channel Box again. The inputs are gone, which means the modeling history has been deleted. The result of Delete By Type is shown in Figure 5.30.

FIGURE 5.30
History deleted

THE ESSENTIALS AND BEYOND

In this chapter, you've tackled the cleanup steps that are necessary to prepare your model for rigging. You added some edge loops to help with bending joints, did a cleanup pass to check for stray verts, moved the character into position for rigging, mirrored, and deleted history. Now your character is ready to be rigged.

ADDITIONAL EXERCISES

▶ Sometimes even deleting history won't create a mirror that works correctly. If that happens, you'll have to merge the verts along the centerline by hand. Select each pair of center verts, and then choose Edit Mesh ➢ Merge. Work your way around the centerline of the character, merging as you go. Remember that pressing g performs the last command issued, a handy shortcut when performing repetitive actions.

▶ Create the other eyeball for your character, either by using Create ➢ Polygon Primitives ➢ Sphere or by duplicating the existing eyeball. *DO NOT* use Mirror Geometry, as this will merge the eyeballs together and treat both spheres as one object.

▶ If you duplicate the existing eyeball, use Edit ➢ Duplicate Special ➢ option box, and make sure Duplicate Input Graph is checked. Once you duplicate the eyeball, use the Move tool to move it into the other eye socket.

▶ Make sure your character is facing the same direction as the positive Z axis. This is the orientation that the Autodesk® Maya® software assumes the character is in for rigging. If your character is facing another way, turn it so it's facing the same direction as positive Z, and do another Modify ➢ Freeze Transformations to zero out the rotation values.

CHAPTER 6

Surfacing Your Character

Thus far, your character has been a uniform gray, the default surface that the Autodesk® Maya® program assigns to all new geometry. Very few animated characters are that color, however. To change the color of your character, you'll create shaders in a process known as *surfacing*.

▶ **Creating a surface**

▶ **Laying out UVs**

▶ **Texture mapping**

Creating a Surface

You can create two types of surfaces: those with a uniform color, and those that use texture maps to add variety and detail to your character. Texture maps are covered later in the chapter; before you can tackle them, you need to know how to create surface types.

Using the Hypershade Window

The Hypershade window is a very powerful and flexible tool for creating surfaces for your model. The following steps show you how to create a basic colored surface:

1. Open your model from the end of Chapter 5, "Modeling with Polygons, Part 3," or use Ch6Start.ma.

2. Choose Window ➤ Rendering Editors ➤ Hypershade, as shown in Figure 6.1.

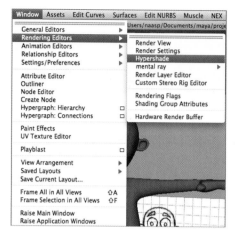

FIGURE 6.1   Hypershade menu item

3. The Hypershade window opens, as shown in Figure 6.2. On the left are the different types of shader bases you can use for your surface, and on the right are two windows that show the shaders currently in the scene (on top) and the shader currently being worked on (at the bottom).

FIGURE 6.2   Hypershade window

4. Create a new lambert surface by clicking the Lambert button on the left side of the Hypershade window, as shown in Figure 6.3. The new lambert surface is added to the shader list, and a thumbnail view of the surface is loaded into the work area at the bottom right of the Hypershade window.

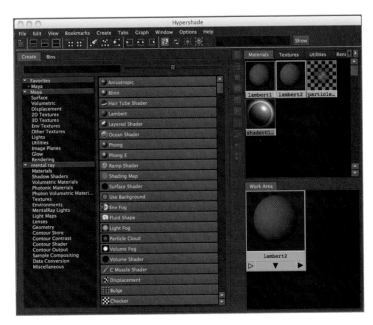

FIGURE 6.3   Creating a new lambert surface

5. Scale the Hypershade window (using the standard method for scaling windows in your operating system) so you can see the main Maya window. Open the Attribute Editor window by clicking the button at upper right in the main window. The Attribute Editor shows the new lambert2 surface, as shown in Figure 6.4.

FIGURE 6.4   Hypershade and Attribute Editor windows

6. Under Common Material Attributes, click the swatch next to the Color attribute. A Color History window opens, as shown in Figure 6.5.

FIGURE 6.5 Color History picker window

7. Select a new color for lambert2, and then roll your cursor off the Color History window to close that window. The thumbnails in the Attribute Editor and Hypershade work area change to reflect the shader's new surface color, as shown in Figure 6.6.

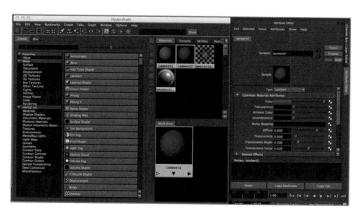

FIGURE 6.6 lambert2 with a new surface color

8. Move (and scale if necessary) the Hypershade window so you can see your model in the main Maya window. Middle-mouse-click `lambert2` in the Work Area window of the Hypershade window, and drag your cursor over the model. Release the middle mouse button (MMB). The `lambert2` shader is applied to the model, as shown in Figure 6.7.

FIGURE 6.7   lambert2 applied to the model

9. In the Attribute Editor, highlight the *lambert2* text and change the name of the shader to **modelSurface**, as shown in Figure 6.8. Notice that the shader name on the tab in the Attribute Editor and in the Work Area window of the Hypershade changed as well.

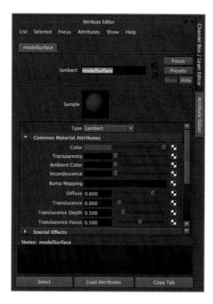

FIGURE 6.8   Shader name changed

Using the Marking Menu

Another way to create and assign shaders to a surface is to use the marking menu:

1. In the Perspective view, click one of the eye spheres to select it, and then right-click over the eye to bring up the marking menu.

2. Select Assign New Material, as shown in Figure 6.9.

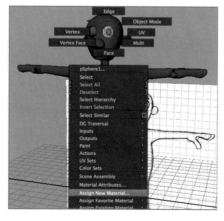

FIGURE 6.9   Assign New Material option
in the marking menu

3. The Assign New Material: pSphere1 window opens, as shown in Figure 6.10. Click the Phong E option.

FIGURE 6.10 Assign New Material: pSphere1 window

Phong and Phong E surfaces have a specular component, which gives the shiny quality that an eyeball would have. Lambert surfaces don't have a specular component.

4. The Assign New Material: pSphere1 window closes, and the Attribute Editor opens. As you did previously, click the swatch next to the Color attribute, and select a color for the eyeball. As you change the color by using the Color History window, the surface of your model changes as well. When you selected Assign New Material, the material shader was assigned to the surface, and any changes to the shader are automatically shown on the surface. Figure 6.11 shows the result of the color selection. Rename the surface eyeball.

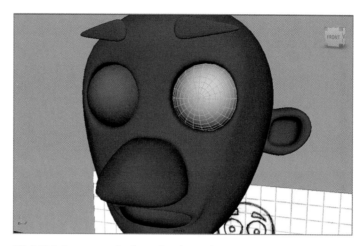

FIGURE 6.11   Surface color changed

5. Select the other eye, and right-click to bring up the marking menu. Select Assign Existing Material a eyeball, as shown in Figure 6.12. The surface of the geometry now has the eyeball material applied to it.

You can assign shaders to individual faces as well as whole models. You will do this later in the chapter. Right-click the model, choose Face, and select the faces to which you want to assign the shader.

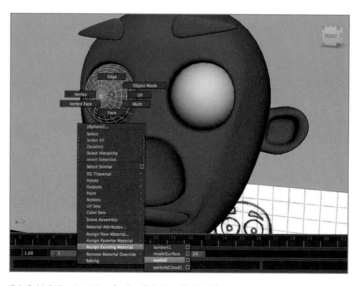

FIGURE 6.12   Assign Existing Material

Laying Out UVs

Frequently you'll want to have more than just a solid color on some or all of your model's surface. You may want to add details such as a name patch, a pants pocket, or some other detail that is too time-consuming or difficult to model into the character's geometry. One technique you can use to add detail to your model is *texture mapping*, whereby you create and assign a picture to the surface of the model. This picture provides the detail that isn't in the geometry itself. Before you create a texture map, you have to lay out your model's UVs.

Understanding the UV Space

UVs are like vertices, except UVs occupy a 2D space rather than a 3D one as vertices do. Think about a box of cereal you buy at the store. When you get the box, it's three-dimensional with pictures and text on it telling you what's inside. That box, however, started out as a flat sheet of cardboard on which the image was printed. Then the cardboard was folded into the 3D shape you see at the store.

The *UV space* is a 2D space where you lay out UVs so they're flat and can be more easily textured. Laying out your UVs in the UV space allows you to put a complex image onto the surface of the model. Figure 6.13 shows the UV space in Maya.

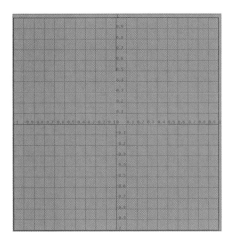

FIGURE   6.13   UV space

Performing the UV Layout

UVs are automatically created as you model, but frequently they're not arranged in a usable layout. Figure 6.14 shows the default UV layout of the model in the Ch6Start.ma file.

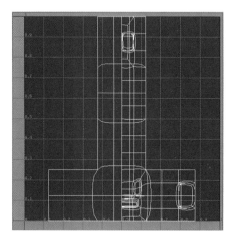

FIGURE 6.14 Default UV layout

As you can see, it's impossible to tell which UVs correspond to which part of the model. Follow these steps to lay out your model's UVs so you can tell which ones are which:

1. Right-click the view window presets (just below the toolbox), and choose Persp/UV Texture Editor, as shown in Figure 6.15. Your view windows now show a Perspective window and the UV Texture Editor window.

FIGURE 6.15
Persp/UV Texture Editor layout selection

2. Click the model. In the Polygons menu set, choose Create UVs ➤ Planar Mapping ➤ Option Box, as shown in Figure 6.16.

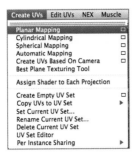

FIGURE 6.16
Create UVs menu

3. The Planar Mapping Options window opens, as shown in Figure 6.17. In the Project From options, select Z axis. Make sure Keep Image Width/Height Ratio is checked, and click the Project button.

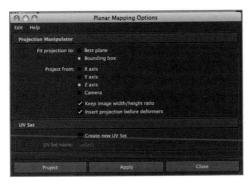

FIGURE 6.17 Planar Mapping Options window

4. The planar projection manipulator appears around the model, and the UVs in the UV Editor window are laid out to reflect the projection, as shown in Figure 6.18.

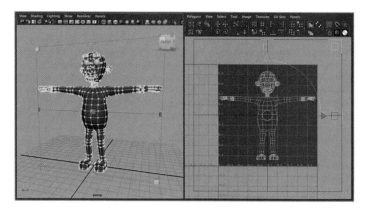

FIGURE 6.18 UVs projected (reference planes turned off for clarity)

With a planar projection, the UVs on the front of the model overlap the ones on the back. Usually that's undesirable, because it means the texture map is the same for all UVs that overlap. To keep that from happening, each set of UVs (known as a *shell*) should occupy its own area in the UV space. (In some cases, having UVs overlap is fine, such as when two parts of the model share the same texture.) To select, scale, and move a UV shell, follow these steps:

> If the projection manipulator disappears, make sure the model is selected, and then go to the Channel Box and click polyPlanarProj1 under INPUTS.

1. In the Perspective window, right-click the model, and select Face from the marking menu. If the model is still in Smooth Proxy mode, press 1 to switch to Polygon mode.

2. Select the faces on the hands and wrists, as shown in Figure 6.19.

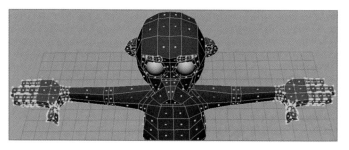

FIGURE 6.19 Hand faces selected

3. Press Shift and the right angle bracket key several times to expand the selection to include the whole arm, as shown in Figure 6.20.

4. Choose Create UVs ➢ Planar Mapping ➢ Option Box, select Y Axis from the Project From options, and click the Project button. Your arm UVs are projected as shown in Figure 6.21.

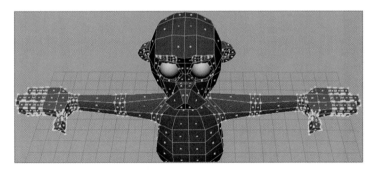

FIGURE 6.20   Selection expanded

Pressing Shift and >
expands your selection,
and pressing Shift and
< contracts it.

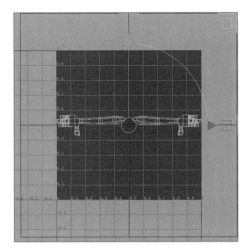

FIGURE 6.21   Arm UVs projected

5. Click the yellow arrow in the UV window, and drag the arm UVs up to
   the top of the UV space, as shown in Figure 6.22.

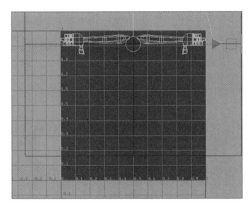

FIGURE 6.22   Arm UVs moved

6. Click anywhere in the Perspective view to deselect the projection. Your UV Editor window should look something like Figure 6.23.

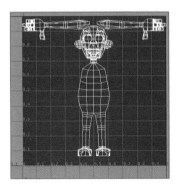

FIGURE 6.23   Revised UV space

7. You can place the UVs for the arms on top of each other, because they'll share the same texture map. This also frees some of the UV space for other projections, as well as saves you time in painting your textures. In the UV Editor window, right-click the arm UV shell on the left, and select UV from the marking menu, as shown in Figure 6.24.

8. Drag to select a few UVs in the arm shell, and then right-click again and choose Select ➢ Select Shell, as shown in Figure 6.25.

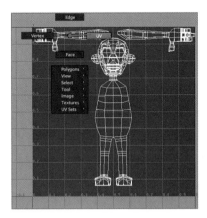

FIGURE 6.24   Marking menu in UV Editor window

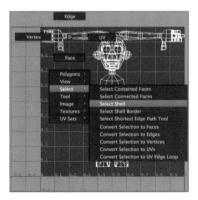

FIGURE 6.25   Selecting the UV shell

9. With all the UVs in the shell selected, right-click the shell, and choose Polygons ➢ Flip ➢ Option Box, as shown in Figure 6.26.

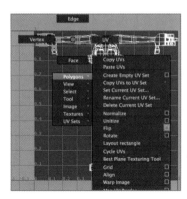

FIGURE 6.26   Polygons a Flip menu option

10. The Flip UVs Options window opens, as shown in Figure 6.27. Make sure Horizontal is selected, and then click Apply And Close.

FIGURE 6.27   Flip UVs Options window

11. The UV shell flips horizontally and highlights. Click anywhere in the Perspective window to deselect the shell and show all the model's UVs in the UV Editor.

12. Repeat step 8 to reselect the UV shell. Press w to select the Move tool, as shown in Figure 6.28.

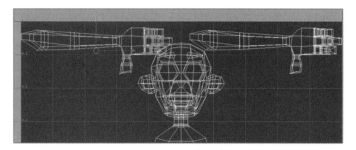

FIGURE 6.28 Shell selected, Move tool active

13. Click the red arrowhead, and drag the flipped shell on top of the other arm shell, matching them as precisely as you can. Your UV Editor window should look something like Figure 6.29.

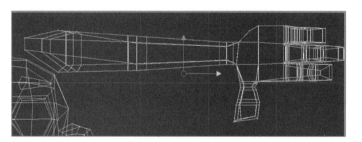

FIGURE 6.29 UV shell moved

14. Continue selecting groups of faces and projecting planar UVs to separate overlapping UVs. When you're finished, your UV space should look something like Figure 6.30.

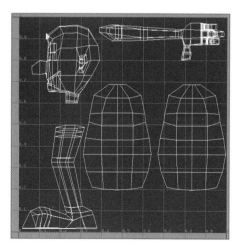

FIGURE 6.30   Completed UV projections

As you project your UVs, each set automatically fills the UV space, overlapping some of the other UV shells. You need to scale them down. To do so, select the shell as you did in the preceding steps, press r to activate the Scale tool, and use the center handle to scale the shell proportionately.

15. To export an image of your UV layout for use in Photoshop or another paint program, select your model in Object mode in the Perspective view. Then, in the UV Editor window, choose Polygons ➤ UV Snapshot, as shown in Figure 6.31.

FIGURE 6.31
UV Snapshot menu option

16. The UV Snapshot window opens. Set the Size X and Size Y options to 2048, as shown in Figure 6.32. Select Targa as the Image Format, and click OK. The UV snapshot is sent to the images folder in the project directory for your scene. The default name for the image is outUV.

FIGURE 6.32   UV Snapshot window

Texture Mapping

To create your texture map, you load your outUV image into a paint program such as Adobe Photoshop, Corel Painter, or the open source GNU Image Manipulation Program (GIMP), and create an image to be applied to your character, using the outUV image as a guide. It's beyond the scope of this book to provide instruction on using paint programs; loads of good books, videos, and tutorials are available on the subject. This section provides a general overview of how to put a texture map together, as well as specific instructions on how to import a texture map into your scene and apply it to your character.

Creating a Color Map

A *color map* is what the name suggests: a texture map that provides the color for your model. The following procedure describes how to create a color map in general terms:

1. In a paint program (Photoshop, Painter, and so forth), open your outUV image. Figure 6.33 shows outUV.tga open in Photoshop.

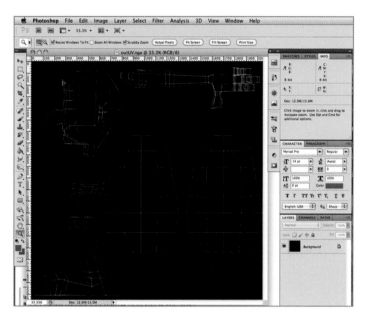

FIGURE 6.33 outUV.tga in Photoshop

2. Create a new layer in the paint program, and begin creating your texture. Figure 6.34 shows a color map in progress.

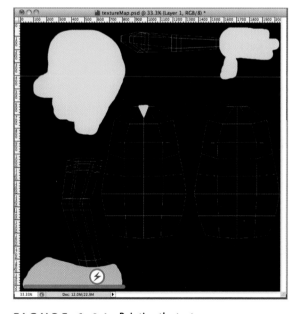

FIGURE 6.34 Painting the texture

Be sure you overpaint a little when creating your textures. The texture map has to come to the edge of the UV shell in order to fully cover the model. So, it's usually a good idea to go a little beyond the edge of the UV shell, just to be certain there are no gaps in your texture map.

3. Your color map can be as simple or as complex as you like. When you're finished painting, save your file in the sourceimages directory for your project. Figure 6.35 shows a simple color map.

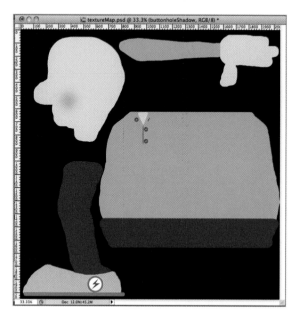

FIGURE 6.35 Completed color map

If you work in Photoshop to create your color map, take advantage of layers and save your final image as a PSD file. Maya can import PSD files, and any changes you make to the color map file automatically appear in the Maya scene.

Applying Your Color Map

Now that you have a color map, it's time to apply it to the character and see the result:

1. In Maya, click the character model.

2. In the Attribute Editor, locate the modelSurface tab and click it. You may have to use the left and right arrows next to the tabs, as shown in Figure 6.36.

3. Click the checkerboard button next to the Color attribute. The Create Render Node window opens, as shown in Figure 6.37.

FIGURE 6.36 modelSurface
tab in the Attribute Editor

FIGURE 6.37 Create
Render Node window

4. Click on the type of file you created (in this example, PSD File). The Attribute Editor window changes to show a psdFileTex1 tab, as shown in Figure 6.38.

If your texture is saved as a file type other than a PSD, click on the File button, and select your texture file.

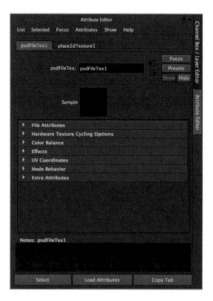

FIGURE 6.38 psdFileTex1 tab

5. Click the arrow next to File Attributes to open that section of the Attribute Editor window (if it's not already open), and then click the folder icon next to the Image Name field. The Open window opens, as shown in Figure 6.39.

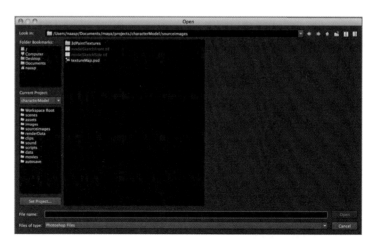

FIGURE 6.39 Open window

6. Select your color map, and click the Open button. Your map is loaded into the Image Name field, as shown in Figure 6.40.

FIGURE 6.40 Color map loaded

7. In the Perspective view, choose Shading ➤ Hardware Texturing, as shown in Figure 6.41.

FIGURE 6.41
Selecting Hardware Texturing

8. Click the model to select it. In the Attribute Editor, click the model-Surface tab, and change the name of the surface in the Lambert field to **finalSurface**. Save your file.

Your texture should appear on the model in Perspective view. By laying out your UVs and using that layout as a guide to painting your textures, the textures appear correctly on the model when you assign the color map to the surface. Figure 6.42 shows a smoothed version of the model with the texture applied.

If your texture map doesn't appear, it could be due to your system's RAM (not enough to display the texture) or your video card. To see the texture on your model, click the small clapboard icon at the top of the screen. Clicking that icon renders a frame of your scene, which lets you see the texture.

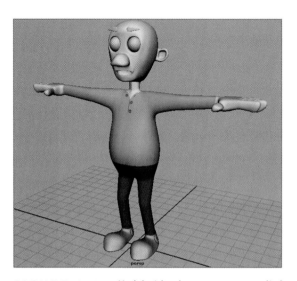

FIGURE 6.42   Model with color texture map applied

Applying Additional Surfaces

Your model can have more than one surface applied to the geometry. You probably noticed that the character's eyebrows and the inside of his mouth are the same color as the rest of the head. To correct this, you can create additional surfaces and apply them to those specific parts of the model:

1. Using the marking menu, select the faces that make up the eyebrows, as shown in Figure 6.43.

2. As you did earlier in the chapter, right-click to bring up the marking menu, and select Assign New Material.

3. Select a Lambert surface.

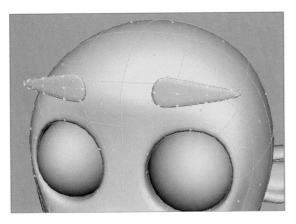

FIGURE 6.43   Eyebrow faces selected

4. In the Attribute Editor, click the color swatch, and pick an eyebrow color you'd like to use.

5. Rename the surface **eyebrow**. Figure 6.44 shows the eyebrows colored and the surface name changed.

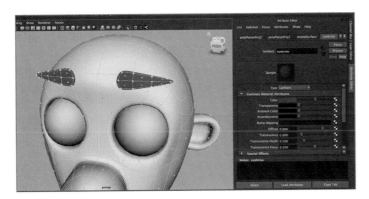

FIGURE 6.44   Final eyebrow color

6. Reposition your Perspective view so you can see into the character's mouth, and select the four faces across the back of the mouth.

7. Hold down the Shift key, and press the right angle bracket once to expand the selection to include all the faces in the mouth interior.

8. Repeat step 2–5, but this time select a Phong E surface and rename your new surface **MouthInt**.

9. Save your file. A smooth proxy view of the textured and surfaced character is shown in Figure 6.45.

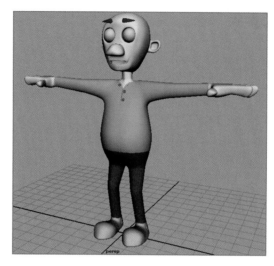

FIGURE 6.45 Model with multiple surfaces

THE ESSENTIALS AND BEYOND

Having a good UV layout is essential to being able to surface your model well. By laying out your UVs and creating a texture map, you can add detail to the model that may not exist in the geometry itself.

ADDITIONAL EXERCISES

▶ Create a UV layout and color map for the eyes. One map will probably do for both eyes, although each eye needs its own UV layout.

▶ Try using some of the other UV projection types that are available and see what results they create. A cylindrical projection, for example, is good to use on features such as the arm and torso, whereas a spherical projection may be a good choice for the head.

▶ Once you apply your texture map and look at the smooth proxy, you may find areas where the surface isn't as you expected it to be. Feel free to go back and change your UV layout to address these issues.

CHAPTER 7

Getting Bent Out of Shape: Blend Shapes

The next step in preparing your character for animation is to create a deformer set and attach it to your main model. Deformers, known in Autodesk® Maya® software as *blend shapes*, change the surface topology of your model in ways you can mix, match, and control.

▶ **Understanding blend shapes and how they work**

▶ **Creating deformers for your character**

▶ **Setting up the blend shape interface**

Understanding Blend Shapes and How They Work

Blend shapes are frequently used for creating facial expressions—smiles, frowns, eyebrow raises, blinks, and so on. They are essentially copies of your main character geometry with specific, focused changes to a small part of the geometry.

Deformer Order

A quick word about deformer order: Maya uses multiple types of deformers to alter your model's geometry, and the order in which those deformers are applied makes a difference. Maya goes through the deformers in the order they were applied, and later deformers can override earlier deformers if they perform similar alterations.

The two main deformer types you'll apply to your model are blend shapes and the skeleton you create in Chapter 8, "Dem Bones: Setting Up Your Joint System," and you should create them in that order. The skeleton won't affect what you're doing with the facial expressions, but the facial blend shapes will definitely influence how the skeleton affects the model. It's possible to reorder the deformers, but it's easier to create them in the right order in the first place.

Blend Shapes

Each vertex in your model has a unique number assigned to it, and the verts are numbered in a particular order. Blend shapes work by checking the position of the verts in a given blend shape and adjusting their position relative to that vert's position in your main model.

Because of this, it's vital that you not add geometry to or delete geometry from either the main model or any of your blend shapes after you've created your blend shapes. If you do add or delete geometry, the vert numbering changes, and the blend shapes will no longer work. If you need to make changes to your geometry, you must do it before you create your blend shapes. For example, you'll add a couple of edge loops to your existing model in order to give you some additional geometry to work with:

1. Open your character model file from the end of the preceding chapter, or use Ch7Start.ma.

   You don't need the image planes anymore, so choose Edit ➢ Delete All By Type ➢ Image Planes to remove them from the scene.

2. Add an additional edge loop around the eye sockets, as shown in Figure 7.1.

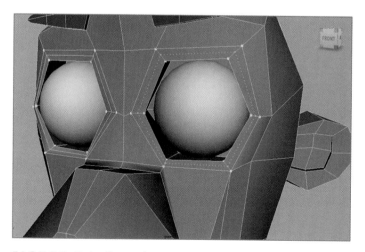

FIGURE 7.1   New eye loop

3. Add an additional loop around the mouth area, as shown in Figure 7.2.

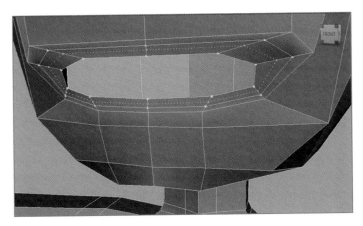

FIGURE 7.2   New mouth loop

4. Clear the modeling history by choosing Edit ➤ Delete By Type ➤ History, as shown in Figure 7.3.

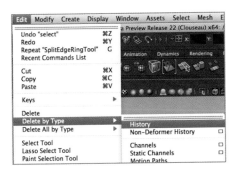

FIGURE 7.3   Deleting history

Creating Deformers for Your Character

Now that you have the geometry set, you can start creating your blend shapes. To do that, you need to plan an approach for creating specific, flexible shapes that you can use in various combinations.

Planning for Facial Deformers

In general, blend shapes work best when they're not trying to do too much. Typically, you make blend shapes that focus on moving one small aspect of the facial geometry rather than trying to create an entire expression at once. For example, you can create blend shapes that move the corner of the mouth up and down, and others that open and close the mouth, rather than creating one blend shape that creates an open-mouth smile. It may seem like more work to create focused, specific blend shapes, but the end result provides more flexibility and options in how the blend shapes are used.

To prepare for creating blend shapes, make a list of the kind of movements you need in your facial features. The example in this chapter focuses on the mouth, so a list of mouth shapes might look like the following:

- ▶ Mouth corner up
- ▶ Mouth corner down
- ▶ Mouth corner in
- ▶ Mouth corner out
- ▶ Upper lip up
- ▶ Upper lip down
- ▶ … and so on

You'll also create blend shapes for the eyebrows, so create a list of possible blends:

- ▶ Inner brow up
- ▶ Inner brow down
- ▶ Mid brow up
- ▶ Mid brow down
- ▶ Outer brow up
- ▶ Outer brow down

Creating Your Facial Blend Shapes

To create your mouth blend shapes, perform the following steps:

1. Select the model in Object mode.

2. Rename the model **Base** by using the Channel Box, as shown in Figure 7.4.

FIGURE 7.4
Base model renamed

3. Choose Edit ➤ Duplicate, as shown in Figure 7.5.

FIGURE 7.5
Duplicating the Base model

4. Select the Move tool (w key), and move the copy of the model to the right of the original, as shown in Figure 7.6.

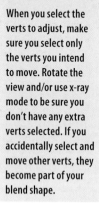

Because the eyeballs are separate objects and will be animated as part of the main model, you don't have to copy them for your blend shapes.

FIGURE 7.6   Model copy moved

5. Zoom in on the mouth area of the copy, and select the vertices at the corner of the mouth on the character's left side (screen right), as shown in Figure 7.7.

When you select the verts to adjust, make sure you select only the verts you intend to move. Rotate the view and/or use x-ray mode to be sure you don't have any extra verts selected. If you accidentally select and move other verts, they become part of your blend shape.

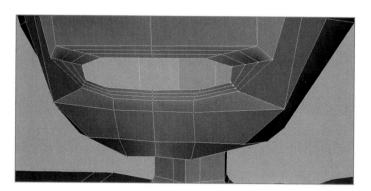

FIGURE 7.7   Vertices selected

6. Move the verts, both as a group and individually, to move the corner of the mouth up, as shown in Figure 7.8.

7. Select the model in Object mode, and rename it **mouthCnrUpLt** in the Channel Box, as shown in Figure 7.9.

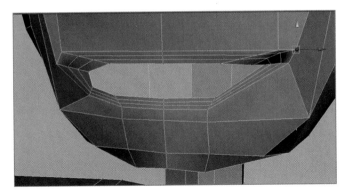

FIGURE 7.8   Vertices moved

FIGURE 7.9
Blend shape renamed

8. Select Base, and create another duplicate, this time by pressing Command/Ctrl + D.

9. Move the duplicate over so it's next to mouthCnrUpLt, as shown in Figure 7.10.

It's important to rename your blend shapes as you go. The name the blend interface displays for each shape is the name assigned to the geometry. It's also important to establish a naming convention that efficiently describes what the blend shape does and to use that convention throughout.

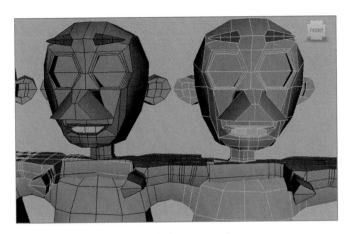

FIGURE 7.10   Second duplicate created

10. Repeat steps 5 and 6 on the right corner of the character's mouth (screen left), creating a blend shape that is a mirror of the first one, as shown in Figure 7.11.

It's good practice to create all your duplicates from the Base model. Because Base is the model you want the blend shapes to affect, it's a good idea to create your blends from a direct copy of that model.

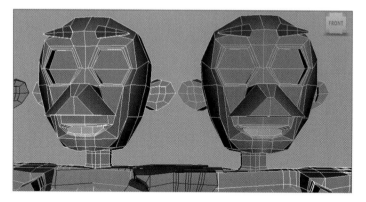

F I G U R E   7 . 1 1   Left and right mouth corner up blend shapes

11. Rename the new blend shape **mouthCnrUpRt** in the Channel Box, as you did for the previous blend in step 7.

12. Create two more duplicates from Base, and adjust the verts at the corners of the mouth to move them down, as shown in Figure 7.12. Name the new blend shapes **mouthCnrDnLt** and **mouthCnrDnRt**.

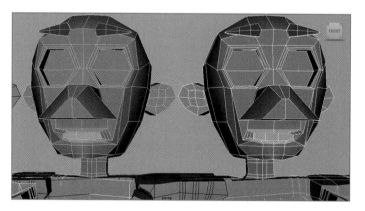

F I G U R E   7 . 1 2   Left and right mouth corner down blend shapes

13. Continue duplicating the original geometry and creating blend shapes for your mouth. Some suggestions for additional blends are as follows:

- ▶ Upper lip up

- ▶ Upper lip down

- ▶ Lower lip up/down

- ▶ Corner in (toward center of mouth)

- ▶ Sneer (using the verts between the center of the mouth and the corner)

14. Once you have the mouth blends you want, create some blends for the eyebrows. This eyebrow set will give you great flexibility and expression:

- ▶ Inner brow up (left and right)

- ▶ Inner brow down (left and right)

- ▶ Mid-brow up (left and right)

- ▶ Mid-brow down (left and right)

- ▶ Outer brow up (left and right)

- ▶ Outer brow down (left and right)

Figure 7.13 shows a selection of blend shapes for the mouth and brows, with the original Base model highlighted on the far left of the top row. Looks a little like a chorus line, doesn't it? As you can see, the number of models you need for creating blend shapes can add up quickly.

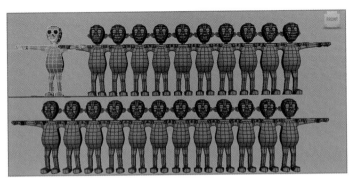

FIGURE 7.13 Blend shapes created

Setting Up the Blend Shape Interface

After you have all your shapes created, it's time to create the blend shape interface that will allow you to apply one or more blends to the main model. To create the blend shape interface window, follow these steps:

1. Select your blend shapes one at a time, Shift-selecting as you go. Finally, select your Base model. Figure 7.14 shows the results of the selection process.

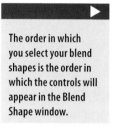

The order in which you select your blend shapes is the order in which the controls will appear in the Blend Shape window.

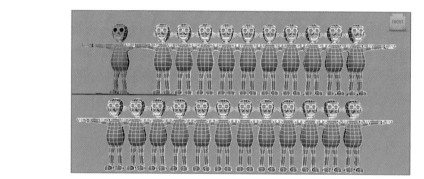

FIGURE 7.14   Blend shapes and Base selected

2. Switch to the Animation menu set, as shown in Figure 7.15.

FIGURE 7.15
Animation menu set

3. Choose Create Deformers ➢ Blend Shape, as shown in Figure 7.16.

4. Click anywhere in the scene to deselect the blend shapes and the Base model.

5. Select the Base model, and press f on the keyboard to zoom in on the model. Then zoom in closer on the face.

FIGURE 7.16
Creating the blend shape interface

6. Choose Window ➤ Animation Editors ➤ Blend Shape, as shown in Figure 7.17.

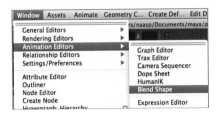

FIGURE 7.17 Blend Shape menu selection

7. The Blend Shape window opens, as shown in Figure 7.18.

FIGURE 7.18 Blend Shape interface window

8. Move the Blend Shape window so you can see your Base model.

9. Move the sliders in the Blend Shape window, and observe how the sliders affect the Base model, as shown in Figure 7.19. The model is in smooth proxy mode to better show the results of the blend shapes.

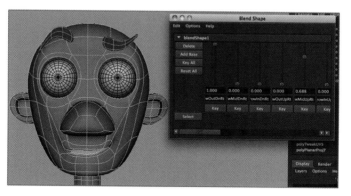

FIGURE 7.19   Blend shapes applied to the Base model

THE ESSENTIALS AND BEYOND

Blend shapes are one type of deformer you can use to affect the surface of your model. With the blend shapes you created, you can animate facial expressions. Animating facial expressions is covered in Chapter 12, "Making It Move: Animating Your Character."

ADDITIONAL EXERCISES

▶ After you've created your blend shape interface, you can delete the blend shape models from your file, and the blend shapes will continue to work. Be sure to save a copy of your file containing the blend shape models in case you need to make changes.

▶ You can add new blend shapes after the interface is created. Create your new blend shape from a copy of the Base model, as before. Select that new blend shape and then the Base model, and then choose Edit Deformers ➢ Blend Shape ➢ Add.

▶ You can also create new blend shapes from your existing blend shapes! Move the sliders in the Blend Shape window to generate the expression you want to make into a blend shape, and then select your Base model and duplicate it. The duplicate will have the expression you created "baked in." Add the new blend shape to the interface as described in the preceding bulleted item.

CHAPTER 8

Dem Bones: Setting Up Your Joint System

Now that your blend shapes are complete, you can add the skeleton, or joint system, to the model. The skeleton's job is to animate larger segments of your character, such as the arm or the head.

▶ **Understanding how joints work**

▶ **Building joint chains**

▶ **Putting it all together**

▶ **Putting it to use: connecting the joints to your model**

Understanding How Joints Work

Joints in a 3D model work pretty much like joints in your body do—you rotate a joint, and some portion of your body moves as a result. However, in a 3D model you can have joints rotate in ways that they never could in your body. You can have an elbow joint that rotates in more than one direction, for example.

Joints function by influencing vertices on the surface of the model. Typically, joints are used for rotation and mimic the joints in a human or animal body. Although they can be used for translation, this happens rarely.

Joints have the potential to influence *any* vertex on the surface of your model, no matter how far the vertex is from the joint. Therefore, you have to take care in setting up your skeleton, as you will in this chapter, and in *weighting* the vertices to the joints in your model, as you will in Chapter 9, "Weighting Your Joints."

Building Joint Chains

Joint chains—like weighting and rigging, which are discussed in later chapters—can get very complex. The details of building a complex skeleton can (and do) fill an entire book. The concepts presented here are the essentials you need to know to build a basic skeleton.

You're going to build a few joint chains, name the joints, and place them in various sections of the model as you go. You build the skeleton in pieces by using these joint chains so they're easier to place in the parts of the model they're designed to influence.

Picking the Correct View for a Chain

When you're creating a joint chain, you should carefully pick the view in which you create that chain. You want to select the view that provides the most information about where the joints in that chain should be positioned. Typically, this is the view that shows the most detail about a feature in the model. For that reason, you will use the Side view to create the spine/neck/head joint chain, as well as the leg chain. For the arm/hand chain, you will use the Top view. Both views are shown in Figure 8.1.

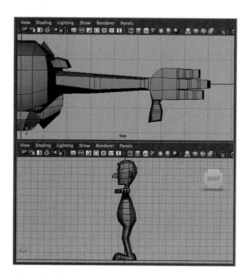

F I G U R E   8 . 1   Views used to create joint chains

Starting in the Middle (of the Character)

The first joint chain you'll create is the chain for the spine, neck, and head. This is the chain all the other chains will hook into to create the overall skeleton, so it's a good place to start. Follow these steps:

1. Open your file from the end of the preceding chapter, or use
   Ch8Start.ma.

2. Place the cursor in the Perspective window, and tap the spacebar to go to a four-panel view. Place the cursor in the Side view, tap the spacebar again to maximize the Side viewport, and zoom in on the model so the torso and head fill the viewport, as shown in Figure 8.2.

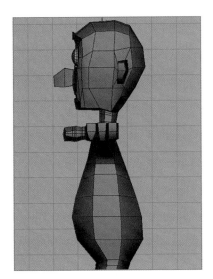

To match the look of the illustrations in the rest of the chapter, select Shading ➢ Wireframe on Shaded in the Side viewport.

FIGURE 8.2 Side viewport maximized

3. Turn on X-Ray view by choosing Shading ➢ X-Ray or by clicking the X-Ray button, both shown in Figure 8.3.

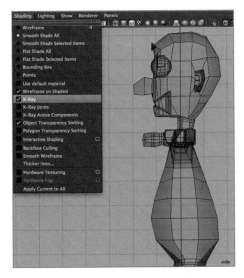

FIGURE 8.3 X-Ray view

4. Switch to the Animation menu set, shown in Figure 8.4.

FIGURE 8.4
Animation menu set

5. Choose Skeleton ➤ Joint Tool, as shown in Figure 8.5.

FIGURE 8.5
Joint tool

6. In the Side viewport, place the crosshair cursor at the character's pelvis area, and click to create a joint, as shown in Figure 8.6.

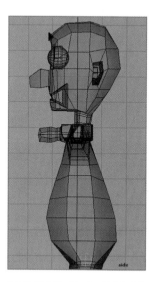

FIGURE 8.6   Pelvis joint positioned

7. Continue up the character, placing three or four joints in the torso area, as shown in Figure 8.7.

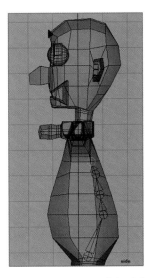

Place your joints where you want the rotation to occur. This generally means you need to position them on edge lines and at the points where the model should bend. That's why you placed the spine joints closer to the back of the model.

FIGURE 8.7 Spine joints positioned

8. Place a joint at the base of the neck, another at the base of the head, and a final joint at the top of the head, as shown in Figure 8.8. When all your joints are in place, press Return/Enter to create the joint chain, as shown in Figure 8.9.

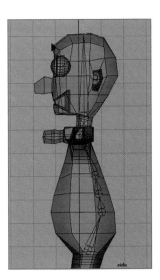

You can adjust the size of the joints in the display by selecting Display ➢ Animation ➢ Joint Size and adjusting the slider to increase or decrease the size of the joint display. This doesn't affect how the joints behave at all.

FIGURE 8.8 Head and neck joints placed

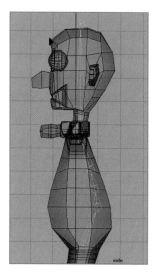

Part of what a joint does is orient the previous joint in the chain. That's why you created a final joint at the top of the head. You won't use this joint for any rotation, but it's necessary to orient the head joint.

FIGURE 8.9 Torso joint chain created

9. Switch to the Front view, turn on X-Ray as described previously, and check to make sure the first joint you created (the pelvis joint) is inside the model geometry. If it's not, select it with the Move tool and move it so that it is. Figure 8.10 shows the pelvis in the correct position.

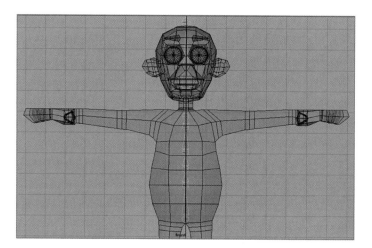

FIGURE 8.10 Pelvis positioned

10. Return to the Side view, and make any necessary adjustments to the joint positions to return them to where you placed them initially. Use the Move tool to position the joints.

Naming Joints

It's important to name joints as you go. Naming joints makes it clear which joint does what and makes it easier to create copies of the leg and arm joints to use on the other side of the character:

1. Select the pelvis joint. The entire joint chain highlights, but only the pelvis joint is actually selected.

2. In the Channel Box, select the joint1 label above the channel values, as shown in Figure 8.11.

FIGURE 8.11
Joint name selected

3. Type **pelvis** to rename the joint and press Return/Enter. The joint is renamed, as shown in Figure 8.12.

FIGURE 8.12
Joint renamed

4. Continue up the joint chain, renaming the joints. In the example, the joints are named spine1, spine2, spine3, spine4, neck, head, and headEnd.

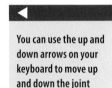

You can use the up and down arrows on your keyboard to move up and down the joint chain.

Creating the Leg Chain

Next, create the joint chain for one leg:

1. Still in the Side viewport, reposition the view so the hip and leg area fill the view, as shown in Figure 8.13.

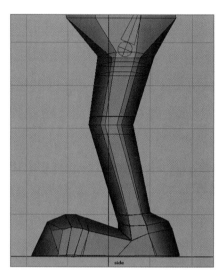

FIGURE 8.13 Leg geometry in Side view

2. Select the Joint tool again by pressing the y key (or from the Skeleton ➢ Joint Tool menu).

3. Being careful not to click the pelvis joint, click to set a joint in the hip area, as shown in Figure 8.14.

4. Work your way down the leg, creating joints for the knee, ankle, foot, toe, and toe end, as shown in Figure 8.15. Press Return/Enter to create the joint chain.

5. Rename the joints as you did with the torso joints. The names used in the example are as follows:

   ▶ hipLt

   ▶ kneeLt

   ▶ ankleLt

- ▶ footLt
- ▶ toeLt
- ▶ toeEndLt

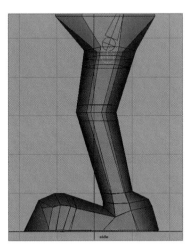

FIGURE 8.14   First leg joint positioned

When you have joints that are repeated on the opposite side of the character, it's important to indicate the side where the joints belong. Naming conventions vary, but they usually include the joint name and either Lt or Rt to indicate which side of the body they're on.

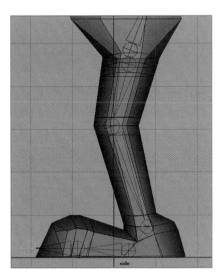

FIGURE 8.15   Leg joints created

6. Switch to Front view. Notice that the joint chain has been created on the 0 Y axis, as shown in Figure 8.16. Select the hipLt joint, and use the Move tool to move the joint chain into the character's left leg geometry, as shown in Figure 8.17.

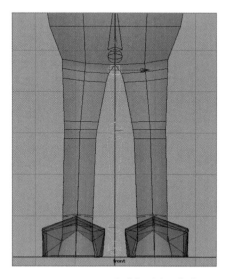

FIGURE 8.16   Left leg joints before move

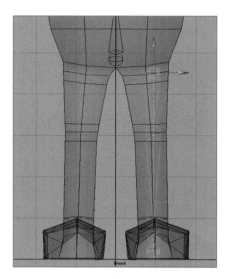

FIGURE 8.17   Left leg joints after move

▶

Don't move any of the leg joints other than the hipLt joint in the Front view. The joints need to stay aligned on the Y axis for the leg IK you'll be setting up in Chapter 10, "Rigging Your Character." *IK*, or *inverse kinematics*, is a technique used to keep parts of the character in place while joints higher up the chain can still be rotated. In this case, the leg joints will be set up with IK to keep the foot in place while the knee and hip rotate.

Creating the Arm Chain

Finally, create a joint chain for the arm and hand:

1. Switch to the Top view. Zoom and reposition the view so the hand, arm, and part of the torso are visible, as in Figure 8.18. As you did in the Side view, turn on X-Ray view.

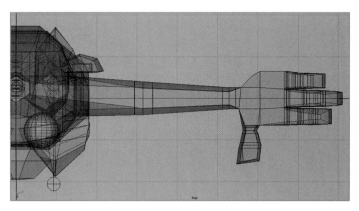

FIGURE 8.18   Top view positioned

2. Select the Joint tool again by pressing the y key (or from the Skeleton ➤ Joint Tool menu).

3. Being careful not to click on any existing joints, click to set a joint in the mid-back area between the spine joints and shoulder, as shown in Figure 8.19. This is your clavicle joint.

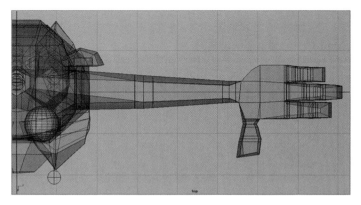

FIGURE 8.19   Clavicle joint created

4. Moving down the arm, create a shoulder joint, an elbow joint, and a wrist joint, as shown in Figure 8.20.

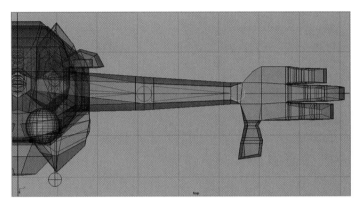

FIGURE 8.20   Shoulder, elbow, and wrist joints created

5. Continue down the hand, creating joints in the middle of the palm and down the middle finger, as shown in Figure 8.21.

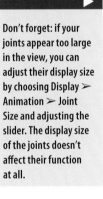

Don't forget: if your joints appear too large in the view, you can adjust their display size by choosing Display ➢ Animation ➢ Joint Size and adjusting the slider. The display size of the joints doesn't affect their function at all.

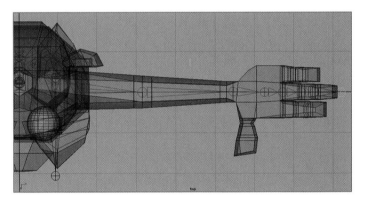

FIGURE 8.21   First hand joints created

6. Press the up arrow on your keyboard to return to the wrist joint. Then begin setting joints again, this time going down the index finger, as shown in Figure 8.22.

7. Press the up arrow on your keyboard to return to the wrist joint again. Then set joints down the little finger, as shown in Figure 8.23.

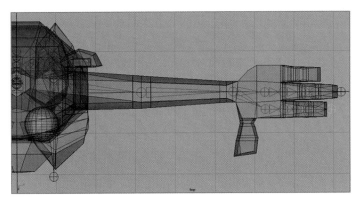

FIGURE 8.22   Index finger joints created

The purpose of the mid-palm joint is to decrease the distance between the wrist and the first finger joint. This makes it easier to set up hand deformations, as you'll do in Chapter 9.

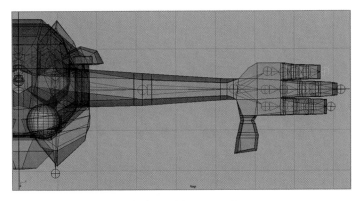

FIGURE 8.23   Little-finger joints created

8. Press the up arrow to return to the wrist again, and create joints for the thumb, as shown in Figure 8.24.

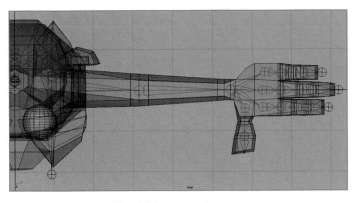

FIGURE 8.24   Thumb joints created

9. Press Return/Enter to create the joint chain, as shown in Figure 8.25.

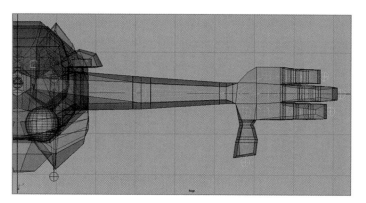

FIGURE 8.25 Arm joint chain created

10. Switch to the Front view, select the shoulder joint, and move the arm joint chain up into the left arm of the model, as shown in Figure 8.26.

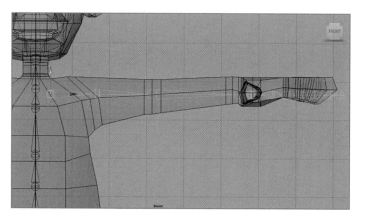

FIGURE 8.26 Arm chain moved

11. As you can see in Figure 8.26, some of the joints aren't in the right position inside the model because of the model's surface. Rotate joints as necessary to get the joints into the center of the model, as shown in Figure 8.27. Rotate on only one axis at a time; and it may be helpful to use the Perspective view, moving around the model for the best view as you work.

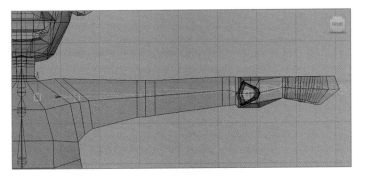

FIGURE 8.27   **Arm chain adjusted**

After you're finished rotating a joint, choose Modify ➤ Freeze Transformations with the joint still selected to reset the joint's rotation value to zero. It's important that the joint's rotation be zero in case you have to reset the joint during animation.

12. Time to rename the joints. Here's a list of the joint names in the example:

   ▶ clavLt

   ▶ shldrLt

   ▶ elbwLt

   ▶ wristLt

   ▶ idxPalmLt (the palm joint for the index finger)

   ▶ idxBaseLt

   ▶ idxMidLt

   ▶ idxTipLt

   ▶ idxEndLt

   ▶ midPalmLt

   ▶ midBaseLt

   ▶ midMidLt

   ▶ midTipLt

   ▶ midEndLt

   ▶ ltlPalmLt

   ▶ ltlBaseLt

   ▶ ltlMidLt

   ▶ ltlTipLt

▶ ltlEndLt

▶ thmbBaseLt

▶ thmbMidLt

▶ thmbTipLt

▶ thmbEndLt

Putting It All Together

Now that you have a named joint chain for the torso and one arm and leg, it's time to create the remaining chains and connect everything into one joint system.

Mirroring Joint Chains

The Autodesk® Maya® software allows you to mirror a joint chain across a specified axis. This saves you the time and trouble of creating duplicate chains for parts like arms and legs. Follow these steps to mirror the chains:

1. In the Perspective view, turn on X-Ray, and zoom in on the character's legs, as shown in Figure 8.28.

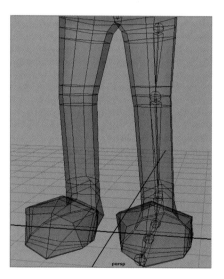

FIGURE 8.28   Preparing to mirror

2. Click the `hipLt` joint, and choose Skeleton ➤ Mirror Joint ➤ Option Box. The Mirror Joint Options window opens.

3. Determine which axis you need to mirror across by looking at the axis widget in the bottom-left corner of the view window. In this example, the axis is the YZ axis (you'll mirror over the axis that runs down the center of your character).

4. Make sure Mirror Function: Behavior is selected, but don't click the Mirror button yet.

Using Variables for Naming

Here's where typing *Lt* over and over again pays off. You can identify a character string within the joint names and have it replaced with another character string. In this case, you will replace *Lt* (for left) with *Rt* (for right):

1. In the Mirror Joint Options window, type **Lt** into the Search For field.

2. Type **Rt** into the Replace With field. The completed window is shown in Figure 8.29.

FIGURE 8.29 Variable names inserted

3. Click the Mirror button. Maya creates a duplicate joint chain inside the right leg of the character, as shown in Figure 8.30, with the joints renamed.

4. Reorient the view window so you can select the `clavLt` joint, as shown in Figure 8.31.

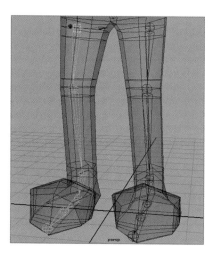

FIGURE 8.30   Mirrored joint chain created

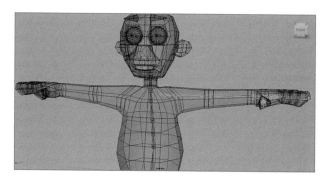

FIGURE 8.31   clavLt joint selected

5. Press g on your keyboard to repeat the Mirror command, and create an arm chain for the right side of your character. The result is shown in Figure 8.32.

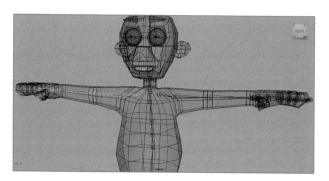

FIGURE 8.32   Right-side arm chain created

Connecting All Your Chains

With all your joint chains created and named correctly, you can now connect them all together into one joint system. Follow these steps to parent the leg and arm chains to joints in the torso chain:

1. Zoom in on the pelvis and hip joints, as shown in Figure 8.33.

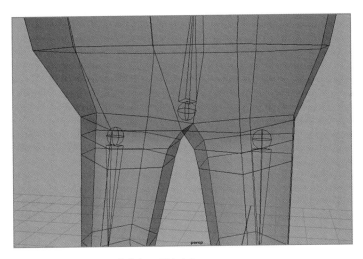

FIGURE 8.33   Pelvis and hip joints

2. Select the hipLt joint, and then Shift-select the pelvis joint, as shown in Figure 8.34.

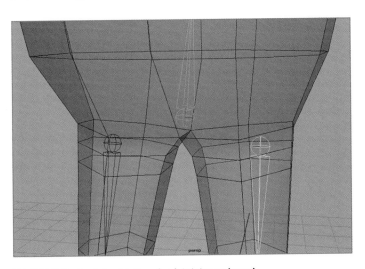

FIGURE 8.34   hipLt and pelvis joints selected

3. Press the p key on your keyboard to parent the hipLt joint to the pelvis joint. The result is shown in Figure 8.35.

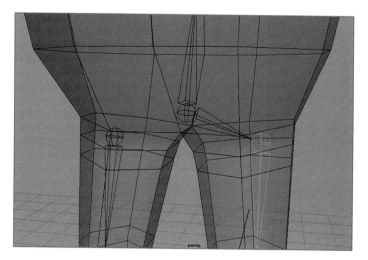

FIGURE 8.35   hipLT and pelvis joints parented

4. Repeat steps 2 and 3 on the right side, parenting the hipRt joint to the pelvis joint. The result is shown in Figure 8.36.

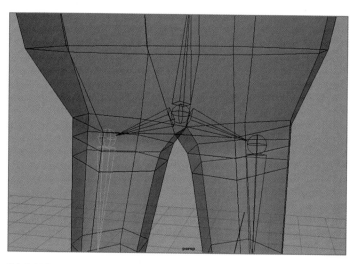

FIGURE 8.36   hipRt and pelvis joints parented

The order in which you select the joints determines which is the parent and which is the child. The pelvis joint should be the parent. You can tell which joint is the parent by determining which joint is next to the large end of the bone geometry. The large end indicates the parent. If the small end of the bone is nearest the pelvis, select the hipLt joint and press Shift + P to unparent, and then try again.

5. Scroll up so you can see both clavicle joints and the top spine joint (the one just before the neck joint). Repeating the process you used in steps 2 and 3, parent the clavicle joints to the top spine joint. The result is shown in Figure 8.37.

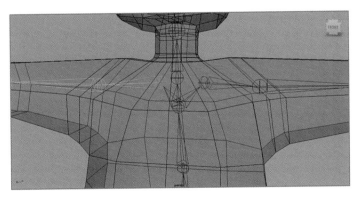

FIGURE 8.37   Clavicle and spine joints parented

6. Your skeleton is now complete. Figure 8.38 shows the model with the skeleton highlighted.

FIGURE 8.38   Completed skeleton

Putting It to Use: Connecting the Joints to Your Model

The joints are now set up in a hierarchy that can control your model's deformation nicely. The final step in this chapter is to attach the joints to the model's geometry, in a process called *skinning*, so rotating a joint causes the model to bend in response. You will also attach the eyes to the skeleton via parenting.

Using Smooth Bind

You will use the Smooth Bind option to attach the joints to the model. Smooth Bind allows any given vertex on the model to be influenced by more than one joint, something that's desirable when you're rigging a character. Frequently you'll want to have more than one joint influence the vertices near a joint so that the bends happen more smoothly and naturally.

Skinning Joints to Your Model

To skin the joints to your model so that rotating a joint affects the model's geometry, follow these steps:

1. Select the `pelvis` joint. Shift-select the character mesh, as shown in Figure 8.39.

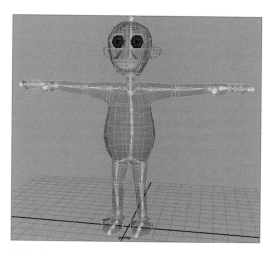

FIGURE 8.39 Skeleton and mesh selection

2. From the Animation menu set, choose Skin ➤ Bind Skin ➤ Smooth Bind ➤ Option Box, as shown in Figure 8.40.

FIGURE 8.40 Selecting the Smooth Bind option box

3. The Smooth Bind Options window opens. Set Bind Method to Closest Distance, set Max Influences to 1, and uncheck Maintain Max Influences. The settings are shown in Figure 8.41.

FIGURE 8.41 Smooth Bind Options settings

4. Click the Bind Skin button.

The character mesh turns purple to show the mesh has been bound to the joints, as shown in Figure 8.42. Click a joint, and then select the Rotate tool and rotate the joint to see how it now affects your model, as shown in Figure 8.43.

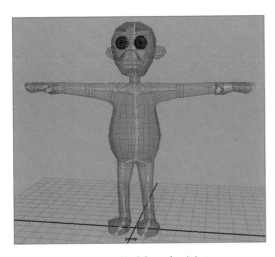

FIGURE 8.42 Mesh bound to joints

Rotate as many joints as you like, but be sure to reset their rotations to 0, 0, 0 when you're finished. There is still more setup to do, and it works best if the joints are in their rest positions when the work is done.

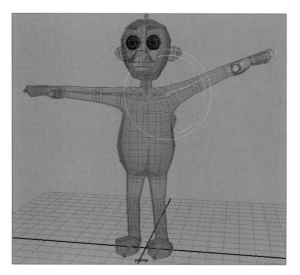

FIGURE 8.43   Joints affecting the model

Parenting the Eyes to the Skeleton

Because the eyes are separate from the main character model, they aren't currently connected to the skeleton. You can parent the eyes to the head joint so that when the head rotates, the eyes move with the head and stay in the eye sockets:

1. Click either eye, and then Shift-click the head joint. The selection should look like Figure 8.44.

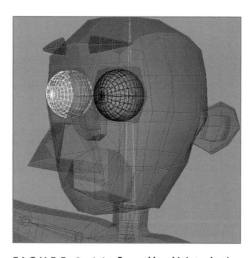

FIGURE 8.44   Eye and head joint selection

2. Press p to parent the eye to the head joint.

3. Repeat steps 1 and 2 for the other eye. Rotate the head joint to ensure that the eyes are parented correctly.

THE ESSENTIALS AND BEYOND

Setting up joints can be a time-consuming, precise task, but it's an important step in the rigging process. Extra time spent getting it right means fewer problems when you start animating your character.

ADDITIONAL EXERCISES

▶ Experiment with the other types of bind options available, and see what kinds of results they produce. For instance, how is the bind different if you choose Closest In Hierarchy instead of Closest Distance?

▶ The Max Influences setting determines the maximum number of joints that can influence any given vertex on a model. You set this to 1 in order to make the weighting steps that follow in Chapter 10 easier to complete. Try setting Max Influences to another number, and then rotate a few joints in your character and see how the character mesh reacts differently.

CHAPTER 9

Weighting Your Joints

After your joints are influencing the surface of your model, they need to be *weighted* so they cause smooth, pleasing deformations when the joints are rotated. This chapter describes how weighting works and how to weight your joints so they deform your model in the way you want.

▶ **Understanding joint weighting and why it's important**

▶ **Adjusting weights**

Understanding Joint Weighting and Why It's Important

Painting skin weights is a vital step in the rigging process. Appropriate skin weights, or the amount of influence a joint has on a given vertex, are crucial in creating a character rig that deforms the model in a pleasing and convincing way.

Joint Influence on Deformation

Every joint in a skeleton has the potential to influence every vertex on the surface of the model. In fact, every joint *does* influence every vertex on the model, but sometimes that influence is zero. The amount of influence a joint has over a vertex will determine how much or how little that vertex moves when the joint is rotated.

Every vertex on the surface of a model must have a *total* influence of 1, or 100%. That influence can be assigned to only one joint, a couple of joints, or many joints, but the total influence on a vertex can be only 1. So if Joint1 has 70% influence on a vertex, and Joint2 has 30% influence on the same vertex, then that vertex will be displaced significantly more when Joint1 is rotated than when Joint2 is rotated. If the influence on a vertex from a joint is 100%, that vertex will move when that joint is rotated, and only when that joint is rotated.

In the Autodesk® Maya® software, one way joint weights are displayed is with a grayscale surface on the character, using black, white, and a range of grays. When vertices have white underneath them, they're influenced 100% by the current joint. When they have black under them, they aren't influenced at all. When the shading under a vertex is gray, it means the selected joint is influencing that vertex at something less than 100%. The closer to white the gray is, the more the joint is influencing the vertex; the closer to black, the less the influence.

Why You Used the Options You Did at the End of the Last Chapter

You'll remember from the end of Chapter 8, "Dem Bones: Setting Up Your Joint System," that you set Max Influences to 1 and turned off Maintain Max Influences. With these settings, every vertex on your model is currently influenced by only one joint, but that influence can be redistributed to more than one joint. This style of binding makes it much easier to redistribute weights over two or more joints. If you had set Max Influences to 2 or higher, there would likely be weight on multiple joints, making it more time-consuming to adjust the joint weights to create smooth, pleasing deformations.

Adjusting Weights

In order to get your model to deform well, you have to make adjustments to the weighting Maya did automatically. Although this is a time-consuming process, the tools Maya provides are easy to use and do the job well. You will use the Paint Skin Weights tool to adjust your weights. To select the tool, choose Skin ➢ Edit Smooth Skin ➢ Paint Skin Weights Tool ➢ Option Box, as shown in Figure 9.1.

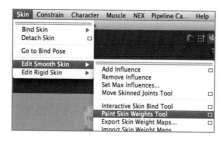

FIGURE 9.1 Selecting Paint Skin Weights tool options

Strategies for Assigning Weights

When assigning and adjusting weights on your model, there are some effective approaches that work very well, get the weights the way you want them, and don't cause additional work for you.

Remember, every vert has to have a total weight of 1. Therefore, it's impossible to "erase" weight by lowering the influence to 0. Any weight you remove from a given vert in this manner has to go to some other joint in the rig, and that's dangerous. You could end up with random parts of your model moving when you rotate the joint, which is undesirable.

To avoid this, a good strategy is to only *add* weight to a vertex, never remove it. If you need to lower the influence of a joint on a vert, select a nearby joint in the chain and add weight to that joint. Adding weight to another joint automatically removes it from the joint with too much influence. In the exercise in this chapter, you'll see this strategy in action. To adjust weight on your model, you'll use two of the paint operations: Add and Replace.

Paint Skin Weights Tool—Add

The Add operation, shown in Figure 9.2, adds the current Value setting, also shown, to the vertex being painted, up to a value of 1. This tool can only increase the value on a vert.

FIGURE 9.2 Paint Skin Weights Add operation

Paint Skin Weights Tool—Replace

The Replace operation, shown in Figure 9.3, replaces the current value on a vert with the value in the current Value setting. This tool can reduce values if the value currently on the vert is higher than the replacement value, so take care that you're replacing with a higher value than the value currently assigned. A good way to check values is with the Eyedropper tool, also shown in Figure 9.3. Click the Eyedropper, and then click the vert you want to check. The Value slider resets to the vert's current value.

FIGURE 9.3   Paint Skin Weights Replace operation

Painting Your Weights

Every character is different, and how the weights on your specific character are distributed will depend on the structure of the model and your goals for how the character will deform. The following exercise shows how to distribute weights and some strategies for working efficiently. To see the example model with completed weights, check out Ch9Finish.ma.

Follow these steps:

1. Open Ch9Start.ma.

2. Select the model geometry.

3. From the Animation menu set, choose Skin ➤ Edit Smooth Skin ➤ Paint Skin Weights Tool ➤ Option Box. The model turns black and white, and the Tool Settings window opens, as shown in Figure 9.4.

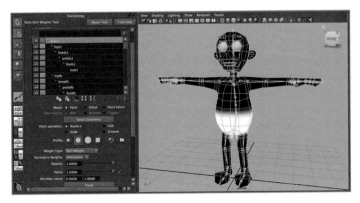

FIGURE 9.4   Paint Skin Weights tool selected

4. Zoom in on the character's left elbow. Select the elbowLt joint from the joint list in the Tool Settings window, as shown in Figure 9.5.

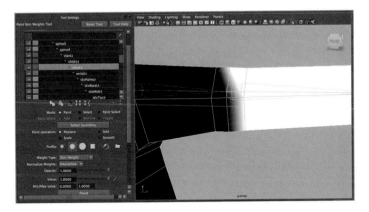

FIGURE 9.5   Left elbow selected

As the figure shows, the elbow influence (white areas) is also distributed to the wrist area, and part of the elbow has no weight at all from the elbow joint (the black area under the verts nearest the shoulder). You'll add some weight to those verts so the verts between the elbow and shoulder are influenced by two joints. You'll also redistribute some weight from the wrist joint to the elbow joint.

5. Near the middle of the Tool Settings window, select the Solid Brush profile, and set Normalize Weights to Interactive, as shown in Figure 9.6. Click Yes in the pop-up window that appears.

FIGURE 9.6 Solid Brush profile selected, and Interactive Normalize Weights selected

6. If necessary, scroll the Tool Settings window and select Replace as the Paint Operation, and set the Value slider to 0.5, as shown in Figure 9.7.

FIGURE 9.7 Selecting the Replace operation

7. Hover your cursor over the character geometry. The brush icon appears—a red circle with an *R* in the center. Reduce the size of the brush by holding down the b key and dragging left until your brush is small enough to touch only one row of verts, as shown in Figure 9.8.

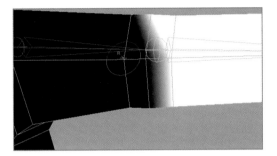

FIGURE 9.8   Sizing the Replace brush

8. Click and hold the LMB, and drag the paintbrush icon over the verts in the elbow edge loop nearest the shoulder. Reposition the view, and paint the weights on the back side of the arm as well. As you paint over the verts, the geometry turns gray, indicating that it is now influenced 50% by the elbow joint. Figure 9.9 shows the completed paint operation.

FIGURE 9.9   Elbow verts painted

9. Reset the Value slider in the Tool Settings window to 1.0, and paint any verts in the next edge loop over (closer to the wrist) that have black beneath them, as shown in Figure 9.10. The completed paint operation for these verts is shown in Figure 9.11.

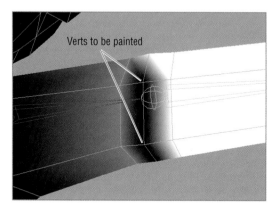

FIGURE 9.10   Unpainted elbow verts

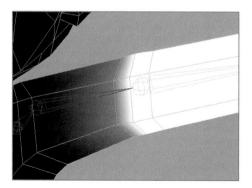

FIGURE 9.11   Painted elbow verts

10. Select wristLt from the Influences list in the Tool Settings window. The wrist loop nearest the elbow should have black under the verts, as shown in Figure 9.12.

11. Reset the Value setting to 0.5 in the Tool Settings window.

12. Hold down the b key, and left-click and drag to resize your brush. Paint the verts in the wrist loop nearest the elbow, as shown in Figure 9.13.

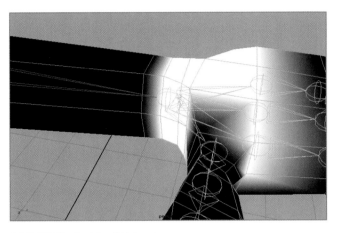

FIGURE 9.12 Wrist verts

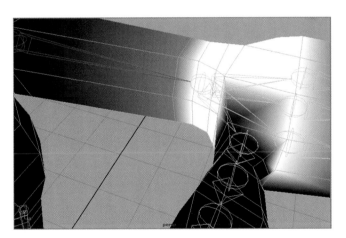

FIGURE 9.13 Wrist verts painted

13. Switch back to the elbwLt joint by using the Tool Settings window, and observe how the verts at the first wrist loop are now gray instead of white, as shown in Figure 9.14. By adding influence to those verts for the wrist joint, you automatically reduced the influence of the elbow joints on the same verts.

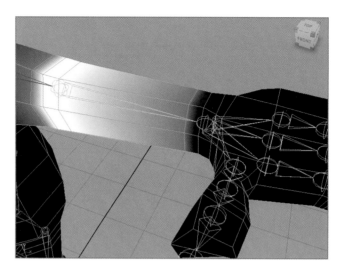

FIGURE 9.14 Elbow loop painting complete

14. With elbwLt selected in the Tool Settings window, click the Lock button at the left side of the window, shown in Figure 9.15. This locks the weights for the elbow as they currently are, so they can't accidentally be changed.

FIGURE 9.15 Elbow weights locked

15. Continue painting weights for every joint on the left side of the character as well as the spine and head. As you get each weight the way you want it, lock the weight to the joint as you did in step 14. To see how the weights are affecting the surface, rotate the joint you're working on and observe the surface deformation. When you're finished checking the rotation, select the model and click the Paint Skin Weights tool icon in the Last Tool Used slot of the Toolbox, as shown in Figure 9.16, and continue weight-painting for any joints that still need adjusting.

Paint
Skin
Weights
tool

FIGURE 9.16
Paint Skin Weights
tool in the Toolbox

Mirroring Weights

Painting weights is a time-consuming, exacting process. Fortunately, you have to paint only half your character, because Maya has a tool that mirrors your skin weights to the other side of the character:

1. Select the model geometry.

2. Choose Skin ➢ Edit Smooth Skin ➢ Mirror Skin Weights ➢ Option Box, as shown in Figure 9.17. The Mirror Skin Weights Options window opens.

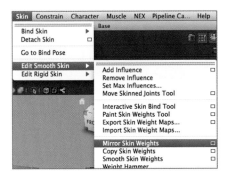

FIGURE 9.17   Mirror Skin Weights Options

3. Select the options shown in Figure 9.18, and then click Mirror. The skin weights on the left are mirrored to the right side of the model.

FIGURE 9.18   Mirror Skin Weights Options settings

In order for Mirror Skin Weights to work, your character has to be centered over the 0 Y axis. If your model isn't in the center of the Maya scene, the mirror function won't find comparable verts on the right side of the model and won't complete successfully.

THE ESSENTIALS AND BEYOND

Skin weighting is a vital part of the rigging process, because it ensures that the surface of the model deforms appropriately. It can be a time-consuming process, but it also can be approached like a puzzle to solve by determining just how much weight from each joint should be applied to each vertex.

ADDITIONAL EXERCISES

▶ One way to speed up the weighting process is to slightly rotate the joint you're working with before weighting. With the joint rotated, you'll see the verts move as you change the weighting, giving you an idea of how the weight you're assigning will affect the surface of the model. After you're finished, be sure to reset the joint to 0 rotation on all three axes.

▶ This process can be overwhelming, especially when you're starting out. If you're having trouble getting your weights the way you want them, try practicing with a cylinder. Create a cylinder with 10–12 loops around the circumference, and put a joint structure inside it, then weight the surface to the joints. Practicing with simpler geometry can make it easier to get the concepts down.

CHAPTER 10

Rigging Your Character

With your skeleton in place and attached to your model, the next step is to rig your character for animation. Character rigging creates controls for making rotating joints easier and speeding up your animation workflow.

▶ **Understanding basic rigging concepts**

▶ **Setting up the leg controls**

▶ **Setting up the torso control**

▶ **Setting up the character control**

▶ **Creating a custom shelf**

Understanding Basic Rigging Concepts

Before you get started, it's helpful to understand the two types of joint rotation you'll be working with: forward kinematics and inverse kinematics. *Kinematics* describes the motion of objects and groups of objects without considering the force that moves those objects—in other words, how the joints in your character rotate, without worrying about what drives that rotation.

Forward Kinematics

Forward kinematics (*FK*) uses a joint higher up the hierarchy to move the joints farther down the hierarchy. For example, the shoulder joint, when rotated, moves the elbow and wrist joints along with the shoulder. FK is automatic when setting up a joint hierarchy—all the joints in your character's skeleton currently use FK for rotation.

Inverse Kinematics

With *inverse kinematics* (*IK*), you use a joint farther down the hierarchy to rotate joints higher up in the joint chain. An IK chain has a defined length, and the joints are all controlled by an IK handle, which when moved rotates the joints in the chain.

IK is great for things like legs, where feet need to stay in place on the ground when a character crouches down. The IK handle is left in place, and by moving or rotating other joints in the model outside of the IK chain, you can bend the character's leg without the foot moving, something nearly impossible to achieve with an FK chain.

Setting Up the Leg Controls

Using IK in a character's legs is a requirement in any rig in order to keep the character's feet in contact with the surface on which he/she/it is standing. You'll use IK chains to set up your character's leg so that it can stay in place and still have the foot and knee rotate as you want them to.

Creating Leg IK Chains

IK chains are relatively straightforward to create. You will use a total of three chains in your character's leg and foot. Follow these steps:

1. Open your weighted character file from the end of the preceding chapter, or use Ch10Start.ma.

2. To make the joint chains easier to see and select, go to the Show menu in the Perspective view, and uncheck Polygons, as shown in Figure 10.1.

FIGURE 10.1
Show ➤ Polygons unchecked

> Character rigs can get very complex. Whole books are written on the process of creating sophisticated rigs. The rig you'll construct here is a simple, functional rig that will familiarize you with basic rigging practices.

3. Zoom in on the left leg joint chain, as shown in Figure 10.2.

FIGURE 10.2   Left leg joint chain

4. From the Animation menu set, choose Skeleton ➢ IK Handle Tool ➢ Option Box, as shown in Figure 10.3.

FIGURE 10.3
IK Handle Tool menu item

5. In the Tool Settings window, select ikRPsolver from the Current Solver drop-down menu, as shown in Figure 10.4.

FIGURE 10.4   ikRPsolver selected

6. Your cursor is now a crosshair. Click the left hip joint, skip over the knee joint, and click a second time on the ankle joint. Your first IK chain is created, as shown in Figure 10.5.

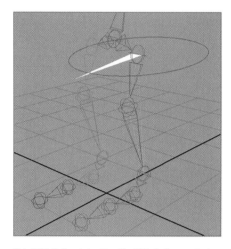

The Rotation-Plane solver allows you to rotate the joint chain. The practical application of this is that you can rotate the knee from side to side. The Single-Chain solver doesn't allow for this kind of rotation.

FIGURE 10.5   First IK chain created

7. Press y on the keyboard to reselect the IK Handle tool. Click the ankle joint, skip over the foot joint, and click a second time on the toe joint. Your second IK chain is created, as shown in Figure 10.6.

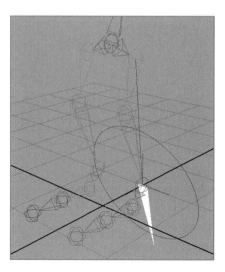

FIGURE 10.6   Second IK chain created

8. Press y to reselect the IK Handle tool. Click the toe joint, and click a second time on the toeEnd joint. Your third and final IK chain is created, as shown in Figure 10.7.

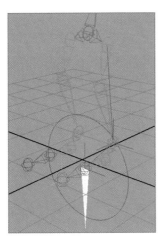

FIGURE 10.7   Third IK chain created

9. Your leg IK chains are complete. If you select all three IK handles (the three-pointed icons that appeared at the end of each chain) and select the Move tool, you can move the foot around, the knee bends in response, and the movement stops at the hip, or the top of the first IK chain. The moved foot is shown in Figure 10.8. After you're finished moving the foot (it *is* fun, isn't it?), undo your moves to return the foot to its rest position.

10. Repeat steps 6–9 on the right leg joints to create IK chains for the right leg.

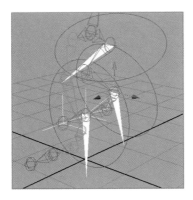

FIGURE 10.8   Leg joints under IK control

Creating an External Control Handle

Selecting all three IK handles on either leg every time you want to move the leg is too time-consuming, so you will create an external control and connect it to the handles. Then, by selecting one control, you select all the handles for a leg with one click. Here are the steps:

1. Turn the model's geometry back on temporarily by clicking the Show menu in the Perspective view and rechecking Polygons, as shown in Figure 10.9.

FIGURE 10.9
Show ➢ Polygons checked

2. Choose Create ➢ NURBS Primitives ➢ Interactive Creation to uncheck that option, then choose Create ➢ NURBS Primitives ➢ Circle, as shown in Figure 10.10.

FIGURE 10.10 Create ➢ NURBS
Primitives ➢ Circle

3. Select X-Ray from the Perspective view's Shading menu to make the model transparent.

4. Move and scale the NURBS circle so that it surrounds the left-foot geometry of the character. When you're finished, you should have something that looks like Figure 10.11.

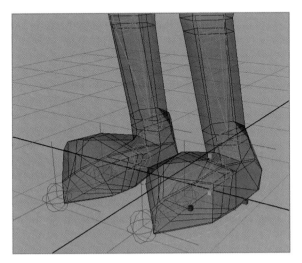

FIGURE 10.11   NURBS circle in place

5. Choose Modify ➢ Freeze Transformations, as shown in Figure 10.12. This zeros out the move information and makes the control easy to reset if necessary.

FIGURE 10.12
Modify ➢ Freeze Transformations

6. In the Channel Box, click the text nurbsCircle1, and rename the circle **footCtrlLt**, as shown in Figure 10.13.

FIGURE 10.13
Foot control renamed

7. Duplicate the circle (Edit ➢ Duplicate), and move the duplicate circle so that it surrounds the right foot, as shown in Figure 10.14. Rename this circle **footCtrlRt**.

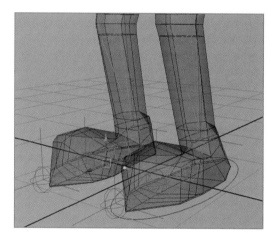

FIGURE 10.14   NURBS circle duplicated and moved

8. Choose Modify ➢ Freeze Transformations to reset the move information to zero.

Connecting the IK Chains to the Handle

To connect the IK chains to the handle you just created, perform the following steps:

1. Uncheck Polygons in the Perspective view's Show menu.

2. On the left leg, click the IK handle at the toeEnd joint, and then Shift-click the IK handle at the toe joint. Press p on the keyboard to parent the toeEnd IK handle to the toe IK handle.

3. Click off the handles to deselect them.

4. Click the toe IK handle, and Shift-click the ankle IK handle. Press p to parent.

5. Click off the handles to deselect them.

6. Finally, click the ankle IK handle, and Shift-click footCtrlLt. Press p to parent the ankle IK handle to the NURBS circle. The NURBS circle now controls all three IK handles.

7. You need to adjust the position of footCtrlLt's pivot point. Select the NURBS circle. Press and hold the d and v keys on your keyboard. The d key activates the pivot point Move tool, and the v key snaps the pivot point to a joint when you move it. With d and v pressed, your pivot point Move tool should look like Figure 10.15.

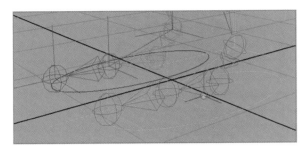

FIGURE 10.15   Pivot point Move tool

8. Click and hold in the center of the pivot point Move tool, and move the pivot point to the ankle joint, as shown in Figure 10.16. Release the d and v keys. The pivot point of footCtrlLt is now at the ankle.

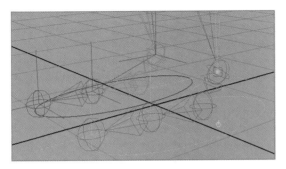

FIGURE 10.16   Pivot point moved

9. Repeat steps 2 through 8 on the right leg.

Using Pole Vector Constraints for Controlling the Knee

Next, you'll create another control and apply a pole vector constraint to it so the knee moves when the control does:

1. Choose Create ➤ Locator, as shown in Figure 10.17.

FIGURE 10.17

Create ➤ Locator menu

2. With the Move tool selected, press and hold the v key to turn on snapping. Click and hold in the center of the Move tool, and move the locator to the left knee, as shown in Figure 10.18.

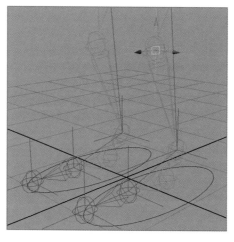

FIGURE 10.18   Locator snapped to the knee joint

3. Using *just* the Z-axis handle, move the locator forward to in front of the knee, as shown in Figure 10.19.

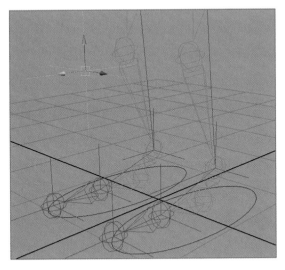

FIGURE 10.19 Locator moved

4. With the locator selected, choose Modify ➢ Freeze Transformations, to zero out the move information.

5. Using the Channel Box, rename the locator **kneeCtrlLt**.

6. With the locator still selected, Shift-click the ankle IK handle and choose Constrain ➢ Pole Vector, as shown in Figure 10.20.

FIGURE 10.20
Constrain ➢ Pole Vector menu

7. A connection is established between the pole vector on the IK handle and the locator, as shown by the line connecting the two. Now, moving the locator rotates the pole vector, which in turn rotates the knee, as shown in Figure 10.21.

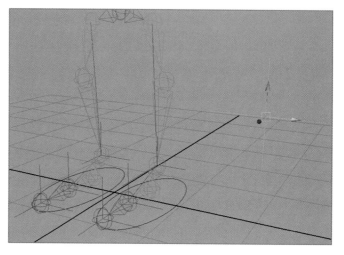

FIGURE 10.21   Pole vector rotated

8. Repeat steps 1 through 6 for the right leg.

Setting Up the Torso Control

Next to the feet, the torso is probably the part of your character you'll move the most. Your next rigging step is to set up a control similar to the foot controls for the torso.

Creating the Torso Control Handle

The torso control attaches to the pelvis joint and allows you to move the character's hips. To create the control handle, perform the following steps:

1. Make the polygons of your model visible by checking Polygons in the Perspective window's Show menu.

2. Create another NURBS circle by using the Create menu.

3. Holding down v to turn on snapping, move the NURBS circle to the pelvis joint.

4. Scale the circle so it's outside the model geometry, as shown in Figure 10.22.

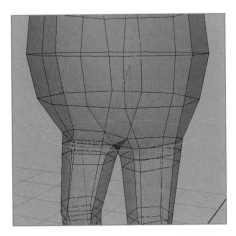

FIGURE 10.22   Torso control scaled

5. Choose Modify ➢ Freeze Transformations to zero out the move information and reset scaling for the circle to 1.

6. Using the Channel Box, rename the circle **torsoCtrl**.

7. Using the Perspective window's Show menu, uncheck Polygons.

Connecting the Torso Control

With the torso control created, the next step is to attach it to the pelvis joint using the following procedure:

1. Select the pelvis joint. Shift-click torsoCtrl, and press p on your keyboard to parent.

2. Test your leg IK. Click torsoCtrl, and move it down toward the feet. The pelvis joint and everything above it should move down, but the feet should stay in place, and the legs should bend as the torso moves down. Figure 10.23 shows torsoCtrl moved downward.

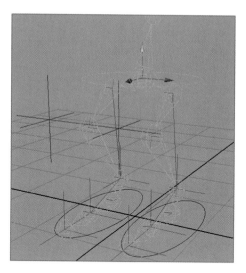

FIGURE 10.23   torsoCtrl moved

3. Reset the Translate values on torsoCtrl to zero using the Channel Box.

Setting Up the Character Control

It's convenient to have one control to click that moves the entire character and all its controls to a new location or positions the character at the beginning of a shot. The final control you'll create moves all the controls at once.

Creating the Character Control Handle

To create the character control handle, which moves the model and all its controls, follow these steps:

1. Create a NURBS circle by using the Create menu.

2. Scale the circle so it encompasses the foot controls, as shown in Figure 10.24.

3. Using the Channel Box, rename the NURBS circle **charCtrl**.

4. Choose Modify ➤ Freeze Transformations to reset the values for the circle.

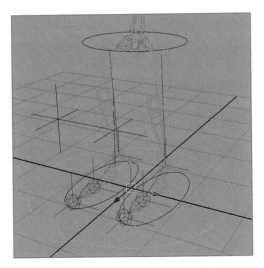

FIGURE 10.24   Character control scaled

Connecting the Character Control Handle

The next step is to connect the character control handle to the rest of your rig. Follow these steps:

1. Select kneeCtrlLt. Shift-click footCtrlLt, and press p on your keyboard to parent the knee control to the foot control.

2. Repeat step 1 for the right knee and foot controls.

3. Select footCtrlLt. Shift-click charCtrl, and press p.

4. Repeat step 3 for the right foot control.

5. Select torsoCtrl. Shift-click charCtrl, and press p.

6. Select charCtrl, and move the character in the scene. All the other controls should move along with the character.

Creating a Custom Shelf

Another way to easily access controls is to create a custom shelf for your character. The following procedure takes you through creating a shelf and button; the number of buttons you create depends on your particular character:

1. Click the small down arrow above the Toolbox window, to the left of the shelf window, and select New Shelf, as shown in Figure 10.25.

FIGURE 10.25
New Shelf menu

2. In the pop-up window that appears, shown in Figure 10.26, type in a name for your new shelf. Click OK.

FIGURE 10.26
Shelf naming window

3. Click the Script Editor button in the lower-right corner of the interface, as shown in Figure 10.27, to open the Script Editor window.

Script Editor button

FIGURE 10.27
Script Editor button location

4. In the Script Editor window, choose Edit ➢ Clear History, as shown in Figure 10.28.

FIGURE 10.28 Clear Script Editor history

5. In the scene window, select the left shoulder joint. A line of code appears in the Script Editor window, as shown in Figure 10.29.

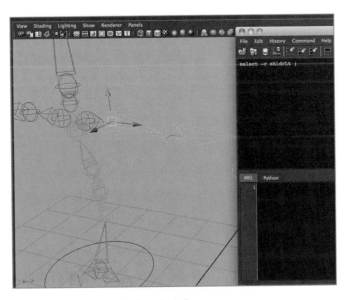

FIGURE 10.29 Joint selected

6. Highlight the line of code in the Script Editor window, and click the Save Script To Shelf button, as shown in Figure 10.30.

FIGURE 10.30
Save Script To Shelf button
location

7. A pop-up window appears, as shown in Figure 10.31. Type **shdLt** in the text field, and click OK.

FIGURE 10.31
Button-naming window

The amount of space for text on a button is very limited. Keep the names you give the buttons as short as possible.

8. Another pop-up window appears, as shown in Figure 10.32. Click the MEL button.

FIGURE 10.32
Script type window

9. The new button appears on your custom shelf, as shown in Figure 10.33. If the button doesn't immediately appear, click the tab for another shelf and then return to your custom shelf.

FIGURE 10.33
New shelf button

10. Click anywhere in the scene to deselect the joint. Click the new shelf button. The left shoulder joint is again selected.

THE ESSENTIALS AND BEYOND

In this chapter, you learned some of the basics of rigging. Rigs can be very simple or mind-bogglingly complex, but they all share the same goal—to make the animation process as smooth and effortless as possible.

ADDITIONAL EXERCISES

▶ You used simple NURBS circles for control handles, but anything can be used as a control. Some handles are shaped like the features they control; others are arrows that show the direction in which the feature can be moved or rotated. Try customizing your controls: select and then right-click the NURBS circle, and select Edit Point. Select an edit point, and use the Move tool to move it around and change the shape of the NURBS circle.

▶ You can use the Create Text menu and icon fonts like Wingdings and Webdings to create interesting-looking controls. Look at the fonts in an application like Photoshop, and see what you could use.

▶ When creating buttons, you can select more than one joint and have those joints combined in one button. The spine joints are good candidates for being selected together. Start with the top spine joint, and Shift-click to select the joints, moving down the spine and selecting the lowest spine joint last. Then, in the Script Editor window, select all the lines that reference the spine, and click the Save Script To Shelf button.

CHAPTER 11

Setting the Scene: Creating an Environment

Your character is now rigged and ready for animation, but he needs some place to show off his moves. In this chapter, you'll create a set for your character, texture the walls and floor, and put in a couple of props to make the room look more interesting.

▶ **Building a Room**

▶ **Building Props**

Building a Room

Building a set in computer graphics is a lot like building a set for a live-action movie: you only build the parts of the set that will be seen on-camera. Not only does this save time and effort, but it also makes camera placement and movement easier, because you're not dealing with walls, furniture, or other elements that may get in the way. For your set, you'll create and texture a side wall, back wall, and floor.

Creating the Floor and Walls

You'll create your set in the scene file containing your character. That way you won't have to import the character later, and you can build your set at an appropriate scale. You'll start by creating the geometry for the floor, then you'll duplicate that geometry, and tweak it for use as the walls, as follows:

1. Open your file from the end of Chapter 10, or use Ch11Start.ma.

2. Select Create ➤ Polygon Primitives, and make sure Interactive Creation is unchecked. If it's checked, select it to uncheck it.

3. Select Create ➤ Polygon Primitives ➤ Plane ➤ Option Box.

4. The Polygon Plane Options window opens. Use the settings shown in Figure 11.1, and click Create.

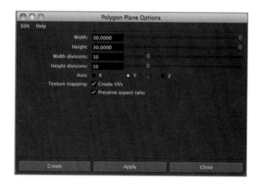

FIGURE 11.1　Polygon Plane Options

5. With the floor plane selected, select Edit ➤ Duplicate. The duplicate will be your back wall.

6. In the Channel Box, set Rotate X to 90, as shown in Figure 11.2.

FIGURE 11.2
Rotating the first wall plane

7. Using the Move tool, position the rotated plane at the back edge of the ground plane, and move it up so the bottom edge is just below the ground plane (see Figure 11.3).

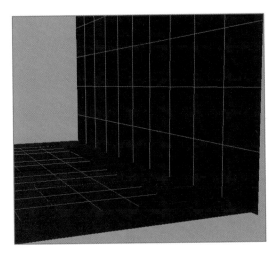

FIGURE 11.3 Back wall plane moved

8. With the back wall still selected, select Modify ➢ Freeze Transformations.

9. Duplicate the back wall, and rotate it 90 degrees on the Y axis.

10. Move the copied wall into position on the screen-left side of the set, as shown in Figure 11.4.

11. With the side wall still selected, choose Modify ➢ Freeze Transformations.

FIGURE 11.4 Side wall created

Texturing the Floor and Walls

With your set walls and floors in place, you can now texture them. The good news is, because they're in their original state, you don't have to lay out UVs for them. You can use a small, tileable texture on the walls and floor, and set the texture so it repeats on the surfaces. Tileable textures are created in a way that makes the edges between repetitions of the texture invisible. Follow these steps:

▶

Loads of free tileable textures are available on the Web. If you don't want to create your own textures, do a search for "tileable textures" or "seamless textures," and pick ones you like.

1. Find or create tileable textures for the wall and floor surface. Figure 11.5 shows a quick wall texture created in Photoshop, along with a floor texture found on the Internet. Place the textures in your project directory's sourceimages folder.

   FIGURE 11.5   Wall texture and floor texture

2. Select and then right-click on the back wall, and select Assign New Material, as shown in Figure 11.6.

3. The Assign New Material window opens. Select Lambert.

4. The Attribute Editor opens, showing the Lambert surface you just created. Click the name field next to Lambert, and change the name to **wallTexture**, as shown in Figure 11.7.

5. Click the checkerboard next to the Color attribute. In the Create Render Node window that appears, click the File button.

FIGURE 11.6 Assign New Material menu item

FIGURE 11.7 Surface renamed

6. In the Attribute Editor, click the folder next to Image Name. Navigate to your sourceimages folder (if necessary), and select your texture map, as shown in Figure 11.8. Click Open.

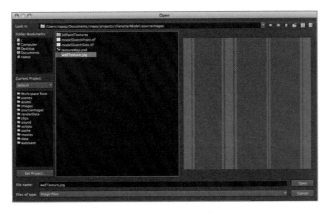

FIGURE 11.8 Texture map selected

7. Turn on hardware texturing by selecting Shading ➢ Hardware Texturing in the Perspective view. The wall texture is visible on the back wall, as shown in Figure 11.9. Currently, the texture is spread over the whole wall. Here's where the repeatable nature of the texture comes into play.

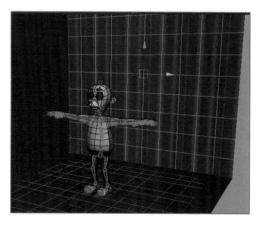

FIGURE 11.9   Texture map placed

8. In the Attribute Editor, click the place2dTexture2 tab. Under 2d Texture Placement Attributes, change the Repeat UV values to something greater than 1. The number you enter in these fields is the number of times the texture will be repeated over the surface of the object. U is the number of repetitions on the horizontal axis, and V represents the number of repetitions on the vertical axis. When you achieve a look that you like, close the Attribute Editor. Figure 11.10 shows the place2dTexture window with Repeat UV values of 5 for the wall texture.

You can change the tiling number at any time by clicking the wall, selecting the wallTexture tab in the Attribute Editor, clicking the button next to the Color field, and then returning to the place2dTexture2 tab.

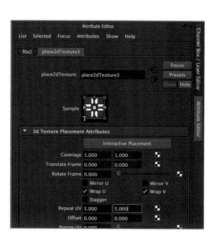

FIGURE 11.10   place2dTexture values

9. To texture-map the other wall, click to select it, and then right-click. Select Assign Existing Material ➢ wallTexture, as shown in Figure 11.11. The texture is assigned to the side wall, as shown in Figure 11.12.

FIGURE 11.11 Assign Existing Material menu item

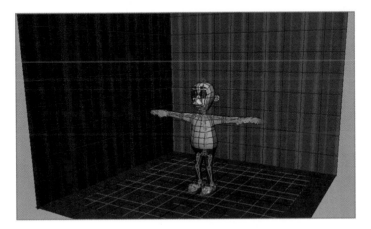

FIGURE 11.12 Texture assigned

10. Select and then right-click the floor plane, and select Assign New Material from the marking menu. Select a Phong E surface, and rename it **floor**.

11. Repeat steps 5 and 6 to assign your texture map to the floor material. Figure 11.13 shows the texture in place (the grid has been turned off to improve visibility).

FIGURE 11.13   Floor texture assigned

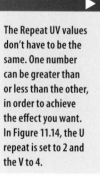

The Repeat UV values don't have to be the same. One number can be greater than or less than the other, in order to achieve the effect you want. In Figure 11.14, the U repeat is set to 2 and the V to 4.

12. Click the place2dTexture3 tab for the floor texture, and change the Repeat UV values until you get a look you like. Figure 11.14 shows the repeat values for the floor texture.

FIGURE 11.14   Floor Repeat UV settings changed

Building Props

You now have a textured room in which your character can perform, but it looks a little bare. Next, you'll create a couple of props to give your set a more lived-in feel.

Creating a Table

You'll build a simple small table and a wall hanging for your set, texture them, and put them in place. First, follow these steps to hide the walls and floor in your scene and make it easier to work on the table:

1. Select the walls and floor of your set.

2. Select Display ➤ Hide ➤ Hide Selection, as shown in Figure 11.15. The walls and floor disappear.

FIGURE 11.15 **Hide Selection** menu item

3. Select Create ➤ Polygon Primitives ➤ Cylinder ➤ Option Box. In the window that opens, set the values as shown in Figure 11.16, and click Create.

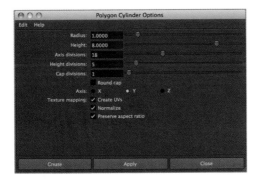

FIGURE 11.16 **Polygon Cylinder Options** window

4. Move the cylinder off to the side of the character. In vertex component mode, move and scale the rings of vertices to create a basic table shape, as shown in Figure 11.17.

FIGURE 11.17
Table sculpted

5. Select Display ➢ Show ➢ All to make the walls and floor visible again. Move the table onto the set, and position it near the side wall toward the back of the set, as shown in Figure 11.18.

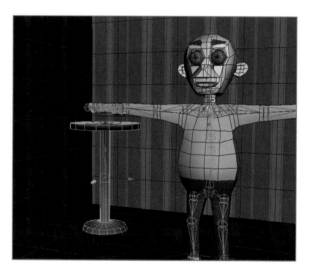

FIGURE 11.18   Table model positioned

6. You will use procedural textures to surface the table. Procedural textures are mathematically generated and don't require image files

to create their effects. Select the faces that make up the tabletop, as shown in Figure 11.19. Right-click to bring up the marking menu, and select Assign New Material.

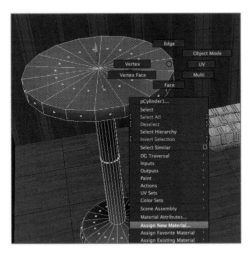

FIGURE 11.19   Tabletop faces selected, and marking menu open

7. The Assign New Material window opens. Select a Phong E material. Rename the material **tableTop**.

8. In the Attribute Editor window, click the checkerboard next to the Color attribute. The Create Render Node window opens, as shown in Figure 11.20. Scroll down the list of materials (if necessary), and select Granite.

FIGURE 11.20   Create Render Node window

9. In the Perspective window, select Renderer ➢ High Quality Rendering to see the texture on your tabletop. In the Attribute Editor, make adjustments to the Granite Attributes until you have a surface you like. Figure 11.21 shows one possible combination of settings.

FIGURE 11.21 Granite attribute settings

10. Select the untextured faces on the table, and assign a new Phong E material to these faces. Rename the material **tableBase**. This time, assign a Wood procedural texture to the Color attribute (review step 8 for details on assigning the surface). As you did in step 9, adjust the surface settings until you have something you like. Figure 11.22 shows one possible combination of settings.

FIGURE 11.22 Wood attribute settings

Creating a Poster

Finally, you'll create a poster to hang on the wall and further dress your set. You will use a photo as a texture map to create the poster's contents:

1. Select Create ➤ Polygon Primitives ➤ Cube ➤ Option Box, and input the values in Figure 11.23. Click Create.

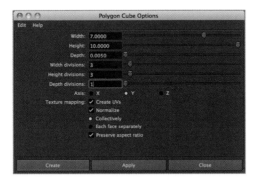

FIGURE 11.23 Poster cube settings

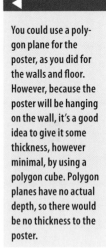

You could use a polygon plane for the poster, as you did for the walls and floor. However, because the poster will be hanging on the wall, it's a good idea to give it some thickness, however minimal, by using a polygon cube. Polygon planes have no actual depth, so there would be no thickness to the poster.

2. Move the cube on the Z axis until it's clear of the floor plane, as shown in Figure 11.24.

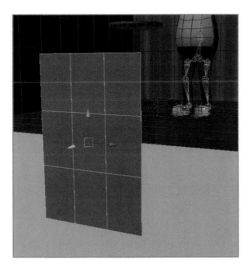

FIGURE 11.24 Poster cube moved

3. Assign a new material to the cube, and make it a white Blinn surface. Rename the surface posterBackSides.

4. In Face mode, select the front faces of the cube, as shown in Figure 11.25.

An easy way to select just the front faces is to click the middle face and then hold down Shift and press the period key one time. This key combination expands the selection to the surrounding faces, selecting the rest of the faces on the front of the cube. If you select too many faces, hold down Shift and press the comma key to contract the selection.

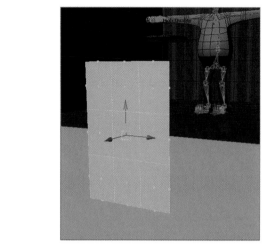

FIGURE 11.25   Front faces selected

5. Assign a new Blinn material to the selected faces. Rename the surface posterFront.

6. With the front faces still selected, choose Create UVs ➢ Planar Mapping ➢ Option Box from the Polygons menu set.

7. Set Project From to Z Axis, as shown in Figure 11.26, and click Project. In the Perspective view, click off the poster to deselect it.

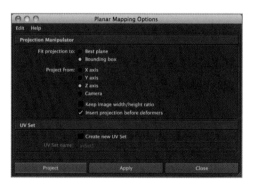

FIGURE 11.26   Planar Mapping Options window

8. Select an image you'd like to have on your poster, and place the image in your project directory's source images directory. The example image used in this tutorial is of the author wearing a Cookie Monster costume.

9. Click the checkerboard next to the Color attribute in the poster-Front surface. Select your image from the sourceimages directory, and click Open.

10. The image loads and appears on the front of the poster. If the image needs to be rotated, click the place2dTexture tab in the Attribute Editor, and use the Rotate Frame slider in the 2d Texture Placement Attributes window to rotate it, as shown in Figure 11.27.

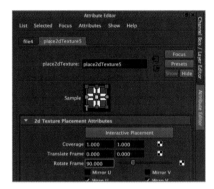

FIGURE 11.27 Rotate Frame control

11. Select the poster in Object mode, and move it to the side wall, rotating it so it's oriented correctly. Figure 11.28 shows the poster in place. Wireframe on Shaded and X-Ray Joints have been turned off, and the hardware render setting has been reset to default quality.

FIGURE 11.28 Poster hung on the wall

◄

Using the orthographic views (Top, Front, and Side) can be very helpful in getting your poster placed exactly as you want it.

THE ESSENTIALS AND BEYOND

In this chapter, you set up an environment for your character to perform in, created new materials and assigned them both texture-based and procedural surfaces, and placed props in the environment to give it a more natural feeling. In the next chapter, you'll bring your character to life by creating a short animated sequence.

ADDITIONAL EXERCISES

▶ Create some additional props to populate your scene. Define a personality for your character, and then think about the kind of things he/she/it would have in a room like this. Would there be chairs? A larger table? More wall hangings? What about little touches, like a flower vase or tableware? Adding details to your scene creates richness and texture in the environment and tells the viewer something about your character.

▶ Several sites on the Internet have premade props and set pieces free for the downloading. Do a search for "Maya models," and see what you find. You can also check out sites like Turbosquid.com and Creativecrash.com, where there are a lot of models aggregated for browsing. In addition to .ma and .mb files, Maya can import several other file types. Select File ➢ Import to open the Import window, and look in the Files of Type drop-down to see the file types Maya can import. Maya can also open .obj files using File ➢ Open Scene. The .obj format is a standard 3D format that practically every 3D application recognizes.

CHAPTER 12

Making It Move: Animating Your Character

It's time to bring your character to life. In this chapter, you'll do some simple animation to get your character moving. The techniques discussed represent the basics of creating animation in Autodesk® Maya® software. Whole books can (and have) been written about animation techniques. The information presented here will get you off to a good start.

▶ **Setting up Maya for animation**

▶ **Animating your character**

Setting Up Maya for Animation

Before you start animating your character, it's a good idea to set up a few options in Maya that will make animating your character easier and more efficient.

Setting Key Tangents

There are as many ways to approach animating a shot as there are animators. One common way uses a technique called *pose to pose*, in which you pose your character on one frame and then create a different pose further along the timeline. To make it easier to see the poses as you work on them, you set the default *out tangents* (the curve type that determines how Maya moves your character) to Stepped. This tangent type holds the pose you set until the playback head reaches the next key, and then the character "pops" into the next pose. Set your tangents by following these steps:

1. Open your file from the preceding chapter, or use Ch12Start.ma.

2. Click the Animation Preferences button in the lower-right corner of the interface, as shown in Figure 12.1.

FIGURE 12.1
Animation Preferences button location

3. In the Preferences window, choose Settings ➤ Animation in the Categories window.

4. In the Tangents section, change the Default In Tangent option to Linear and Default Out Tangent to Stepped, as shown in Figure 12.2. Click the Save button.

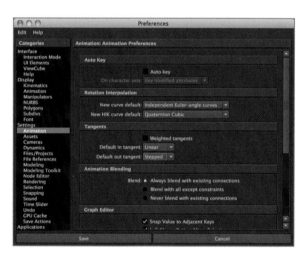

FIGURE 12.2   Default in and out tangents set

Creating a Camera and Turning On the Resolution Gate

When you animate a shot, you always want to animate *to camera*, so you can pick the strongest pose possible. Having a camera created and the *gate* turned on lets you see exactly what your audience will see:

1. Choose Create ➤ Cameras ➤ Camera, as shown in Figure 12.3.

FIGURE 12.3   Create ➢ Cameras menu

2. From the view window menus, choose Panels ➢ Perspective ➢ camera1, as shown in Figure 12.4.

FIGURE 12.4
Selecting the camera1 window

3. The view window switches to the camera1 view. From the view window menu, choose View ➢ Camera Settings ➢ Resolution Gate, as shown in Figure 12.5.

FIGURE 12.5   Turning on the resolution gate

4. A box appears in the view window. Whatever is inside the box is within the camera's resolution. Using the view-manipulation tools, move the camera so that your view window looks similar to Figure 12.6.

When you use the view-manipulation tools in a camera window, you're physically repositioning the camera in the environment. This is a much easier way to frame a shot than moving the camera in a perspective window, because you can see exactly what the camera is seeing as you move it.

FIGURE 12.6   Shot framed

Locking Down the Camera

It's very easy to accidentally move the camera after you have it set up for your shot. To prevent that, you will lock down the camera so it stays in the position you've chosen:

1. In the view window, click the Select Camera button. The box in the camera1 view highlights to indicate that the camera is selected, as shown in Figure 12.7.

Select Camera button

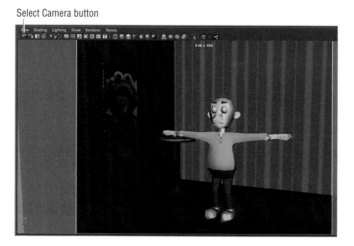

FIGURE 12.7   Select Camera button, and box highlighted

2. With the camera selected, open the Channel Box window (if it isn't already open), and drag-select all the channels for the camera, as shown in Figure 12.8.

FIGURE 12.8
Camera channels selected

3. With the channels selected, right-click any channel name, and choose Lock Selected from the pop-up menu, as shown in Figure 12.9.

FIGURE 12.9
Lock Selected option

4. The value fields for the camera's channels turn gray to indicate they're locked, as shown in Figure 12.10. The camera is now locked down and can't be moved.

If you need to move the camera later, reselect the camera and the channel names as you did earlier, and then right-click a channel name and choose Unlock Selected.

FIGURE 12.10
Camera channels locked

Animating Your Character

A piece of animation goes through several stages from concept to completion. In this section, you explore those stages as you create a simple looping animation, or *cycle*, of the character doing a little hopping dance step.

A *cycle* is any animated clip whose end matches up to its beginning, so it can play endlessly. The simplest example of a cycle is an animated GIF that you might see on a website. More sophisticated examples are character actions in video games or some background character animation in feature films.

Creating a Pop-Thru

The first step in animating your character is creating the main poses for your action. With the out tangent set to Stepped, your character will appear to "pop" from one pose to the next. This action is called a *pop-thru* for that reason. Follow these steps to create a pop-thru:

1. Before you start posing your character, take a little time and work out the main poses with pencil and paper, creating small thumbnail sketches, as shown in Figure 12.11.

FIGURE 12.11   Thumbnail sketches

You don't have to be able to draw well to create thumbnails. Simple stick-figure drawings work very well. It's faster to work out your ideas on paper, trying a few options, before you spend the time and effort posing your character model.

2. Make sure your playback head is on frame 1. In the Perspective view, click the model, and press 3 on your keyboard to switch to Smooth Proxy view.

3. The preceding thumbnails suggest that the character's hands are in a fist. Either by using the shelf buttons you created or by clicking individual joints, form both hands into fists, as shown in Figure 12.12. Remember to press s to set a key for each joint as you rotate them into position.

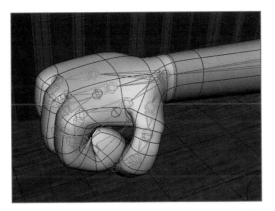

FIGURE 12.12   Finger poses completed

4. Still on frame 1, and using the thumbnail sketch as a guide, use the charCtrl, footCtrl, kneeCtrl, and arm joints to pose your character so that it looks like the first thumbnail sketch. When you're finished, your pose should look similar to Figure 12.13.

FIGURE 12.13
First key pose completed

If you're having trouble selecting the foot controls, you can temporarily hide the floor by selecting it and choosing Display ➤ Hide ➤ Hide Selection.

5. Go to frame 21, and, without changing anything, key all the controls again. You're creating a cycle, and you need to start and end with the same pose.

6. Go to frame 6, and pose your character like the second thumbnail sketch, being sure to set a key for the charCtrl, footCtrl, kneeCtrl, and arm joints. Your second pose should look something like Figure 12.14.

Be sure to set keys for all the controls you're using, not just the ones you're moving for this pose. For example, footCtrlRt needs a key, even though it's staying in place in this pose, because in the next pose you'll move it.

When you move the character up by using the charCtrl, make sure when posing the foot that the footCtrls are in contact with the model. In an IK setup, the IK handles should never be far from the goal object, which in this case are the footCtrls.

FIGURE 12.14
Second key pose completed

7. Go to frame 11, and pose your character like the third thumbnail sketch, being sure to set keys as you go. This is the mirror to the pose on frame 1, but it doesn't have to be exactly the same. Your pose should look something like Figure 12.15.

FIGURE 12.15
Third key pose completed

If you did a Freeze Transformations when you created your `charCtrl` and `footCtrls`, you can reset them to their initial positions by typing **0** into the Translate X, Y, and Z fields in the Channel Box.

8. Go to frame 16, and pose your character like the fourth thumbnail sketch, setting keys as you go. Your character should look something like Figure 12.16.

FIGURE 12.16
Fourth key pose completed

If you'd like to copy your arm poses from frame 6, select a joint, click frame 6 in the timeline, and then right-click and select Copy. Next, click frame 16, right-click, and choose Paste ➤ Paste.

9. Click the button at the right end of the Time Slider, and drag left to shorten the active sequence to 20 frames. To see your key poses in action, click the Play Forwards button to the right of the timeline.

Timing the Pop-Thru

Now that your key poses are done, it's time to let Maya do some inbetweening and get your animation playing smoothly. Inbetweening is where Maya takes the keys you've defined and creates the transitional positions between them:

1. One at a time, carefully select every control and joint that has more than one key set (charCtrl, footCtrls, kneeCtrls, and the clav, shoulder, elbow, and wrist joints).

2. Choose Window ➢ Animation Editors ➢ Graph Editor, as shown in Figure 12.17.

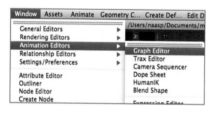

FIGURE 12.17   Graph Editor menu selection

3. The Graph Editor window opens. Press a to make all the animation tangents visible, and then drag-select over every tangent to select them all, as shown in Figure 12.18.

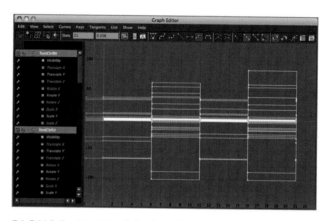

FIGURE 12.18   Selecting all tangents

After you've selected all the keyed controls and joints, you can create a shelf button that selects them all for you. Follow the steps for creating buttons in Chapter 10, "Rigging Your Character."

4. Click the Auto Tangents button at the top of the Graph Editor window, as shown in Figure 12.19. The tangent lines are now curved.

Auto Tangents button

FIGURE 12.19   **Auto Tangents button**

5. Close the Graph Editor window, and click the Play Forwards button to see your animation.

Adding Breakdown Poses

The key poses look good, but when they're inbetweened, you get a result that really wasn't planned. Instead of kicking his foot forward as he lands, the character slides his foot forward after it leaves the ground. To keep this from happening, you will add a couple of keys to further define the character's action. These additional keys are known as *breakdown poses*, because they further break down the action between the keys. Here are the steps:

1. Click the Animation Preferences button in the lower-right corner of the interface. In the Preferences window that appears, choose Settings ➤ Animation from the Categories window, and change the default in and out tangents to Auto, as shown in Figure 12.20. Click the Save button.

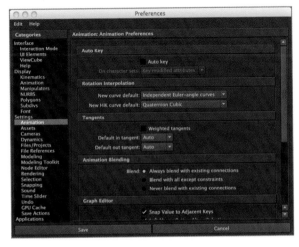

FIGURE 12.20   **Default tangent types changed**

2. Click footCtrlRt, and move the playback head to frame 8.

3. Press w to select the Move tool. Move footCtrlRt back so that the foot is under the torso, as shown in Figure 12.21, and set a key. You may want to work in the Side or Perspective view to best see where the foot is.

FIGURE 12.21 Foot control moved

To get a view setup like Figure 12.21, choose Window ➢ View Arrangement ➢ Two Panes Side By Side.

4. Click footCtrlLt, and move the playback head to frame 18.

5. Repeat step 3 for footCtrlLt.

6. Click the Play Forwards button to see the change in your animation. The feet now stay back longer and kick forward quickly.

7. With the playback head on frame 1, click footCtrlRt.

8. Right-click the playback head, and select Copy.

9. Click frame 3 to move the playback head, and then right-click and choose Paste ➢ Paste. The key information you copied from frame 1 is now pasted on frame 3.

10. Move the playback head to frame 11, and click footCtrlLt.

11. Repeat steps 8 and 9 for footCtrlLt, pasting the copied information on frame 13.

12. Click the Play Forwards button to see your changes. Now the foot pushing off the ground stays in contact longer, giving the action more believability.

Polishing the Animation

Right now, everything in your shot happens at the same time: the arms go down on the same frame that the leg kicks out, for example. In the real world, things don't move like this. Some actions start before others, and other actions end later. In animation, this concept is referred to as *overlap and follow-thru*.

You'll apply some overlap and follow-thru to your character's arm movements to make them feel a bit more believable:

1. Choose the clav, shoulder, elbow, and wrist joints on both arms.

2. Choose Window ➢ Animation Editors ➢ Dope Sheet, as shown in Figure 12.22.

In most character animation, the goal is for the movement to be believable, not realistic. Realistic animation is very difficult to achieve, because of the endless number of subtle movements people make all the time.

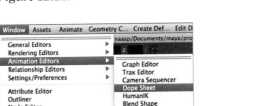

FIGURE 12.22 Dope Sheet menu selection

3. The Dope Sheet opens. Drag-select the elbow and wrist keys, as shown in Figure 12.23.

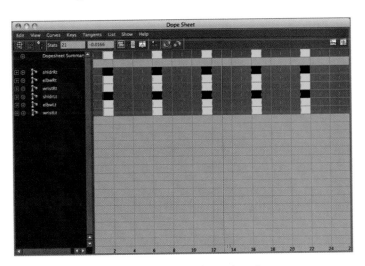

FIGURE 12.23 Elbow and wrist keys selected

4. Press w to select the Move tool.

5. Middle-mouse-click one of the selected keys. A double-headed arrow appears. Drag the keys one frame to the right, as shown in Figure 12.24.

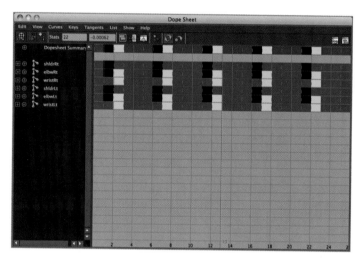

FIGURE 12.24   Keys moved

6. Click off the keys to deselect them, and then drag-select the wrist keys.

7. Middle-mouse-click, and drag the wrist keys one more frame to the right.

8. Click the Play Forwards button to see the result of moving the keys. The arms now have a slightly circular movement, and the wrist action ends two frames later than when the character lands, lending more believability to the action.

9. To add the final touches to your motion, select all the controls that have multiple keys on them, and then open the Graph Editor window (Window ➤ Animation Editors ➤ Graph Editor).

10. Expand the Graph Editor window until you can see the Pre- and Post-Infinity cycle buttons, shown in Figure 12.25.

The process of moving keys to create overlap and follow-thru is known as *offsetting* or creating *offsets*. It's the very last step in the animation process; the keys and breakdowns have to be right before the offsets are done.

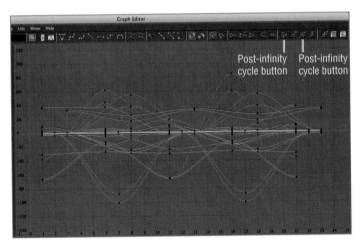

FIGURE 12.25   Pre- and Post-Infinity cycle buttons

11. Press a to zoom out to see all your tangents. Then drag-select all your keys and tangents.

12. With all the keys and tangents selected, click the Pre- and Post-Infinity cycle buttons. Dotted-line tangents appear, as shown in Figure 12.26.

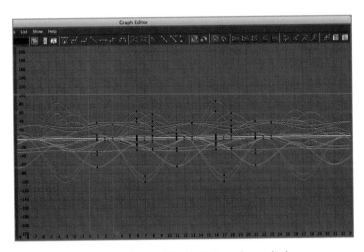

FIGURE 12.26   Pre- and Post-Infinity cycles applied

The Pre- and Post-Infinity cycles continue your actions prior to and after the section of frames you animated. This is handy when you're creating a cycle with offsets, because it ensures that the first frame of the sequence matches up with the last frame so the cycle is smooth.

THE ESSENTIALS AND BEYOND

Animation is a time-consuming process. In this chapter, you created keys, breakdowns, and offsets to create the beginning of a cycle. You also employed Pre- and Post-Infinity cycles to ensure that your action cycles, or loops, correctly.

ADDITIONAL EXERCISES

▶ You can do much more with the animation on this shot. Try animating the head, neck, and spine joints. Be sure frames 1 and 21 are the same on any additional animation you create so that your cycle is smooth and works correctly.

▶ What does this motion look like when you act it out? When animators are trying to work out an action, they will frequently act it out themselves to see how their bodies are moving. Try acting out this action, paying attention to what your body is doing, and add what you discover to your animation.

▶ You can also videotape yourself or a friend performing this action. Sometimes it's easier to figure out what's going on if you can look at a video of the action. Animators frequently use reference footage to break down movement and figure out exactly how to create a believable performance.

CHAPTER 13

Let There Be Light: Lighting Your Shot

Lighting plays a big part in establishing the feel and mood of a scene. Any given scene can be made to look inviting, scary, or any other look you're going for simply by the type, number, and intensity of the lights you place in the scene. The basics of lighting are easy to learn and, once mastered, can be applied to a variety of scenes.

▶ **Understanding the three-point lighting system**

▶ **Using the lights**

▶ **Lighting your scene**

▶ **Performing light linking**

Understanding the Three-Point Lighting System

There are some exceptions, but most scenes are lit with the three-point lighting system. The *three-point lighting system* is a technique for making sure elements of the scene are well lit and stand out from the background. A basic three-point lighting setup is shown in Figure 13.1.

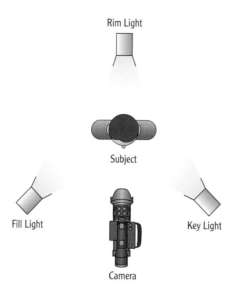

Rim Light

Subject

Fill Light

Key Light

Camera

FIGURE 13.1   Three-point lighting setup

Although any scene can include dozens or even hundreds of lights, each light generally falls into one of three categories:

▶ Key light

▶ Fill light

▶ Rim light

Key Light

The *key light* is the main light in a scene and provides most of the illumination for the scene element it's lighting. The key light is usually placed to one side of the camera and is the brightest light in the scene. Figure 13.2 shows a basic scene lit by a key light.

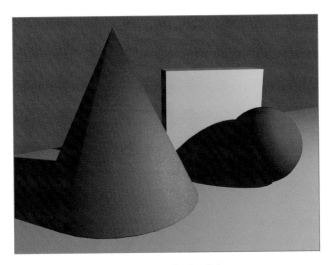

FIGURE 13.2   Scene lit with a key light

Fill Light

The key light does a good job of illuminating the scene but creates some pretty stark shadows. The *fill light*'s job is to put some light in these areas so the scene doesn't look quite so film noir-ish The fill light is usually placed on the opposite side of the camera from the key light, and it's less intense than the key. Figure 13.3 shows the scene with a fill light added.

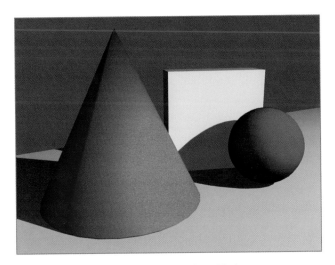

FIGURE 13.3   Scene with fill light added

Rim Light

The *rim light*'s job is to help separate the scene elements from the background. The rim light is placed above and behind the scene and is usually set at a fairly high intensity. Figure 13.4 shows the scene with a rim light added. Figure 13.5 shows the Autodesk® Maya® scene with the camera and light placements.

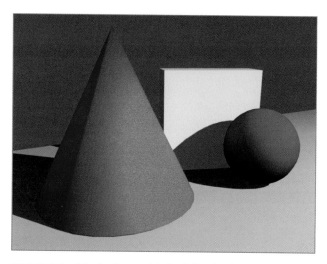

FIGURE 13.4   Scene with rim light added

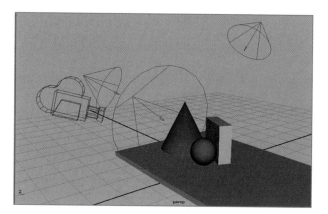

FIGURE 13.5   Lights in a Maya scene

Using the Maya Lights

Maya has several light types, each with different properties and uses. There are three that are the most versatile, and you'll find yourself using them frequently:

- ▶ Directional light
- ▶ Spot light
- ▶ Point light

Directional Light

The best way to think of the *directional light* is as being like the Sun. The Sun's rays travel in all directions, but the Earth is so far away and so small in comparison that when the Sun's light reaches us, the rays are essentially parallel. The directional light is similar: it illuminates everything in the scene (unless you exclude some geometry—more on this later), and the rays travel in parallel. It doesn't matter where the light is in the scene; it only matters which direction the light is pointing. The directional light icon is shown in Figure 13.6, and its effect on the scene is shown in Figure 13.7.

FIGURE 13.6
Directional light icon

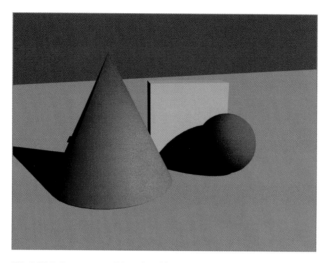

FIGURE 13.7   Directional light in scene

Spot Light

The *spot light* is just like a spot you'd see used on a stage or movie set. It casts light in a given direction and covers a given area; anything outside that area isn't illuminated. The rays cast by the light fan out from the light source in a radial pattern. Figure 13.8 shows the spot light icon, and Figure 13.9 shows the spot light's effect on the scene.

FIGURE 13.8
Spot light icon

FIGURE 13.9 Spot light in scene

Point Light

A *point light* is like a lightbulb. Light emanates from it in all directions, and there are no boundaries on the rays' travel. Think of a point light as a lamp with the shade removed. Figure 13.10 shows the point light icon, and Figure 13.11 shows a scene illuminated by a point light.

FIGURE 13.10
Point light icon

FIGURE 13.11   Point light in scene

Lighting Your Scene

It's time to light your scene. In preparation for doing that, you'll make sure all your scene elements are visible and ready to go.

Placing Your Lights

The first thing to do is make sure all your scene elements are visible, and then you can start creating and placing your lights. Follow these steps:

1. Open your scene from the end of the preceding chapter, or use Ch13Start.ma.

2. Select Display ➢ Show ➢ All, as shown in Figure 13.12.

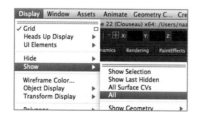

FIGURE 13.12   Display ➢ Show ➢ All menu item

3. Choose Create ➤ Lights ➤ Spot Light, as shown in Figure 13.13. A spot light icon is created at the origin.

FIGURE 13.13 Spot Light menu item

4. With the light still selected, choose Panels ➤ Look Through Selected, as shown in Figure 13.14.

FIGURE 13.14
Look Through Selected
menu item

5. The view switches to show what the spot light sees. The circle in the middle of the view window is the area the spot light illuminates. Using your view-manipulation tools, reorient the view so that it looks similar to Figure 13.15. This is your key light.

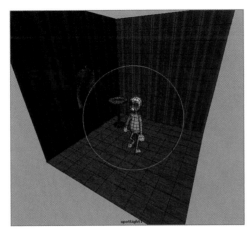

FIGURE 13.15 Key light placed

Remember that your character jumps up in the air during his cycle, so leave some room above the character when you're placing the circle. If you want to check to make sure the spot light will cover him when he jumps, click and hold the playback head and "scrub" back and forth on the timeline to see your animation.

6. Choose Create ➢ Lights ➢ Point Light, as shown in Figure 13.16. A point light is created at the origin. This is your fill light.

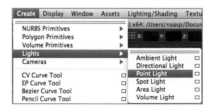

F I G U R E 1 3 . 1 6   Point Light menu item

7. Move the light so it's to the left side of the camera and slightly above it, as shown in Figure 13.17.

F I G U R E 1 3 . 1 7   Fill light placed

8. Create another spot light. Using Look Through Selected as you did with the key light, place it above and behind your character for a rim light. Figure 13.18 shows the view from the spot light's perspective.

Your main lights are now in place. In the next section, you set the intensity of the lights so the scene is lit well.

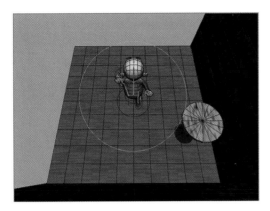

FIGURE 13.18   Rim light placed

Setting the Intensity of Your Lights

Each light will have a different intensity depending on the role it's playing in lighting the scene. Typically, the key light is the brightest, with the fill and rim being somewhat less intense. Follow these steps to set the light intensity:

1. Switch to the Perspective view, and move the view so you can see all three light icons, as shown in Figure 13.19.

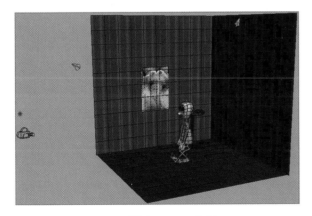

FIGURE 13.19   All three scene lights

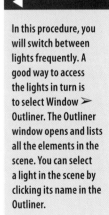

In this procedure, you will switch between lights frequently. A good way to access the lights in turn is to select Window ➢ Outliner. The Outliner window opens and lists all the elements in the scene. You can select a light in the scene by clicking its name in the Outliner.

2. Click each light, and change its name in the Channel Box. Use the names **keyLight**, **fillLight**, and **rimLight**.

3. Select fillLight. In the Attribute Editor, click the fillLightShape tab. Open the Point Light Attributes section, and deselect Illuminates By Default, as shown in Figure 13.20. Doing so turns off fillLight.

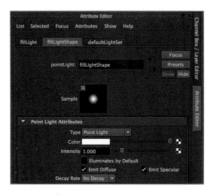

FIGURE 13.20 Turning off the fill light

4. Repeat step 3 for rimLight.

5. keyLight is now the only light illuminating the scene. Select the camera view. From the Rendering menu set, select Render ➤ IPR Render Current Frame, as shown in Figure 13.21.

FIGURE 13.21 IPR Render Current Frame menu item

6. When the Select A Region To Begin Tuning prompt appears in the Render View window, drag a selection box around your character and some of the background, as shown in Figure 13.22.

FIGURE 13.22 IPR render with character selected

7. With the Render View window visible, adjust the Intensity setting for the light in the Attribute Editor until the scene is well lit but not overly bright. The setting used for Figure 13.22 is approximately 1.4.

8. Select fillLight, and recheck Illuminates By Default in the Attribute Editor. The Render View window should immediately show fillLight illuminating the scene. Adjust the intensity level to fill in the shadow areas on the screen-left side of the character. An intensity of about 0.275 works well.

9. Repeat step 8 with rimLight. An intensity of about 0.6 for this scene works well.

10. In the Render View window, click the Render Current Frame button, shown in Figure 13.23. A rendered frame of your scene replaces the IPR render in the window.

Render Current Frame button

FIGURE 13.23 Render Current Frame button

◀

IPR stands for *Interactive Photorealistic Rendering*. It's an interactive window that shows changes to the scene as you make them. It's very handy for setting lighting levels.

◀

If you want to see the effect the light is having on the scene, toggle Illuminates By Default on and off while watching the Render View window.

◀

Your character will look blocky and angular in the render. You will smooth the character in the next chapter before doing your final rendering.

Casting Shadows

Currently, your lights don't cast shadows. The next step is to turn on one of the two shadow options that Maya offers for one or more of the lights in your scene:

▶ *Depth map shadows* use a map (similar to the texture map you created earlier in the book) to create shadows.

▶ *Ray trace shadows* mean the light rays coming from the lights in the scene are tracked, and shadows are created when the rays strike an object.

Follow these steps to create shadows using the depth map option:

1. Select keyLight, and scroll down in the Attribute Editor to the Shadows section. Click the arrow next to Shadows to open the section (if it's not already open), and scroll down to Depth Map Shadow Attributes.

2. Click the Use Depth Map Shadows check box, and set the Resolution to 2048, as shown in Figure 13.24.

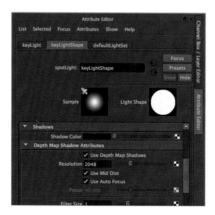

FIGURE 13.24   Depth map shadow settings

3. Click the Render Current Frame button (to the left of the IPR button). A single frame renders, showing the shadow created by the depth map, as shown in Figure 13.25.

FIGURE 13.25   Render with a shadow

4. The shadow is currently pretty hard-edged. To soften the edges of the shadow areas, change the Filter Size setting under Depth Map Shadow Attributes to a higher number. Figure 13.26 shows a shadow with a Filter Size setting of 10.

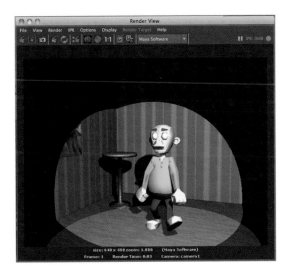

FIGURE 13.26   Shadow with a higher Filter Size setting

5. Add shadows to `fillLight` and `rimLight`, if you like.

Performing Light Linking

One of the great things about lighting in a CG environment is that lights don't have to behave as they do in the real world. As you've seen, lights don't necessarily have to cast shadows. You can set negative values on a light and actually remove illumination from the scene. Another option is to have a light illuminate specific objects in a scene without illuminating others. In Maya, this process is called *light linking*.

In the following steps, you'll see how to unlink a light from an object in the scene:

1. Figure 13.27 shows the still-life scene from earlier in the chapter, lit by a single spot light.

FIGURE 13.27 All scene elements lit

2. To access light linking, in the Rendering menu set choose Lighting/ Shading ➤ Light Linking Editor ➤ Light-Centric, as shown in Figure 13.28.

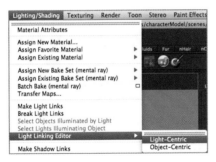

FIGURE 13.28 Light Linking Editor menu item

3. The Relationship Editor window opens with the scene lights in the left column and the scene elements in the right column. By clicking a light to select it, you can see the elements in the scene that light illuminates (see Figure 13.29).

FIGURE 13.29 Relationship Editor with light selected

4. To remove an object from a light's influence, hold down Command/Ctrl and click the object. Figure 13.30 shows the Relationship Editor with the sphere removed from the spot light's influence.

FIGURE 13.30 Sphere unlinked from the spot light

5. The light no longer illuminates the sphere, as Figure 13.31 shows.

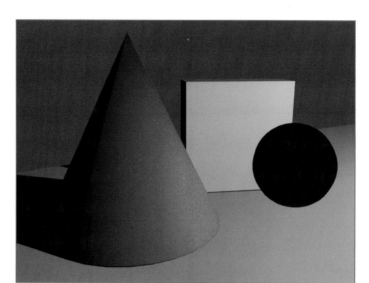

FIGURE 13.31   The sphere is no longer lit.

THE ESSENTIALS AND BEYOND

In this chapter, you lit your scene and learned a little about the three-point lighting system, a standard arrangement for many scenes in movies and games. You also discovered that although lights in a CG environment can behave like lights in the real world, they're also capable of things that real-world lights simply can't do.

ADDITIONAL EXERCISES

▶ Try setting negative values on a light in your scene to see the result. Negative values remove light from a scene and are often used in areas that are over-lit and need to be a bit darker.

▶ Add some additional lights to better illuminate the set as a whole. Use the light-linking technique to keep from over-illuminating your character.

▶ Lights can also be incorporated into set elements. For example, you can create a simple light fixture and put a light inside it to illuminate the image on the wall, or create a candle for the tabletop with a point light inside to suggest the flame.

▶ Lights, like any other objects in a scene, can be animated. Try putting a fourth light in the scene with a very low intensity and animating its translate values to create a moving-light effect.

CHAPTER 14

Rendering and Compositing Your Scene

Now that your animation is complete, it's time to render out the scene and put together a movie file that you can play on your computer, load onto your mobile device, or share on the Web. In this chapter, you'll generate final frames from the animation you created and do some simple compositing to turn those rendered frames into a movie file.

▶ **Making 2D images out of 3D scenes**

▶ **Performing compositing**

Making 2D Images Out of 3D Scenes

Although you've been working in a 3D environment, eventually you have to output your work as 2D images. Even 3D stereoscopic movies use two sets of 2D images per frame to achieve the 3D effect. This section takes you through preparing for and rendering your final frames.

Smoothing Your Model

Throughout producing your shot, you've been working with a low-polygon model. As you probably noticed in your test renders in Chapter 13, "Let There Be Light: Lighting Your Shot," the character looks kind of blocky and chunky. Before you do your final render, you want to smooth out the character so it looks nice and rounded:

1. Open your scene file from the end of Chapter 13, or open Ch14Start.ma.

2. Click the character mesh, and, in the Polygons menu set, choose Mesh ➢ Smooth ➢ Option Box, as shown in Figure 14.1.

FIGURE 14.1 Selecting the Mesh ➢ Smooth option

3. The Smooth Options window opens, as shown in Figure 14.2. Under Exponential Controls, set Division Levels to 2, and click Smooth.

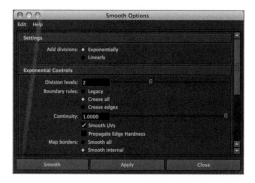

FIGURE 14.2 Smooth Options window

4. The model's geometry becomes more detailed. Click the Rendering shelf tab, and then click the Render Current Frame button, shown in Figure 14.3, to render a test frame and see the smoothed version of your model, as shown in Figure 14.4.

Render Current Frame button

FIGURE 14.3 Rendering a test frame

A point light has been added to the scene and unlinked from the character model in order to provide some fill light for the set.

FIGURE 14.4 Render of the smoothed model

Setting Your Render Preferences

Before you render your scene, you need to check your render settings to make sure the frames you get are usable, the right size, and the right format:

1. Choose Window ➤ Rendering Editors ➤ Render Settings, as shown in Figure 14.5.

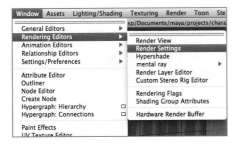

FIGURE 14.5 Selecting the Render Settings menu option

2. The Render Settings window opens. Click the Common tab, shown in Figure 14.6.

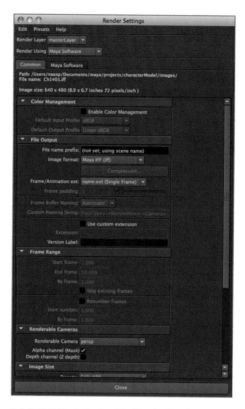

FIGURE 14.6 The Render Settings window's Common tab

3. You need to address several settings on this tab. In the File Output section, type the name you want to use for your image files in the File Name Prefix field. Any name that makes sense to you is fine, and shorter is better.

4. In the Image Format list box, switch the file type to Targa.

5. In the Frame/Animation Ext field, select name#.ext.

6. In the Frame Padding field, set the number to 2. All these changes are shown in Figure 14.7.

7. In the Frame Range section, set End Frame to 20, as shown in Figure 14.8.

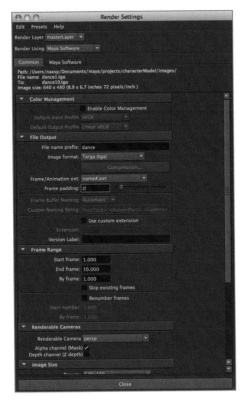

FIGURE 14.7 File output settings

Targa files are good-quality images and render fairly quickly. The name#.ext choice uses the name you selected, the frame number, and the .tga extension as the filename. Frame padding is the number of digits in the frame number and should always be the same as the number of digits in the last frame of your scene.

FIGURE 14.8 Frame Range section

You're rendering only 20 frames because frame 21 is the same as frame 1. Including frame 21 would cause a short pause in the playback loop.

8. In the Renderable Cameras section, set Renderable Camera to camera1, and make sure Alpha Channel (Mask) isn't selected, as shown in Figure 14.9.

FIGURE 14.9 Renderable Cameras section

9. Click the Maya Software tab. In the Anti-Aliasing Quality section, set Quality to Production Quality, as shown in Figure 14.10. Click the Close button.

FIGURE 14.10 Anti-Aliasing Quality section

Running a Batch Render

With all your settings in place, it's time to let your Autodesk® Maya® software generate the final frames you'll use to create your movie file. Follow these steps to run the batch render:

1. In the Rendering menu set, choose Render ➢ Batch Render ➢ Option Box, as shown in Figure 14.11.

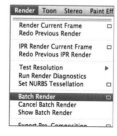

FIGURE 14.11 Selecting the Batch Render option

When rendering, you always want to render individual frames, not a movie file. If problems occur during a render, and you're rendering individual frames, you will only have to re-render a few frames. If you render to a movie file and run into a problem, you have to re-render the entire scene.

2. The Batch Render Animation window opens, as shown in Figure 14.12. Make sure Use All Available Processors is selected, and then click the Batch Render and Close button.

FIGURE 14.12 Batch Render
Animation window

3. The render process begins. You can track the progress of the render in the message window at the lower right of the interface window, as shown in Figure 14.13.

FIGURE 14.13 Render progress

4. When the render is complete, you see the message shown in Figure 14.14. With all your frames rendered, it's time to put your movie file together.

FIGURE 14.14 The Rendering Completed message

Finding Your Frames

When you render your frames, Maya automatically puts them into the images directory of the project directory your scene is in. You can verify that your frames are in the images directory by going to your documents directory and then navigating to maya ➢ projects, selecting the project directory your scene is using, and navigating to the images directory.

Performing Compositing

Compositing is a deep and complex subject, beyond the scope of this book. Generally speaking, compositing refers to taking individually rendered scene elements and combining them into a finished image. For our purposes, *compositing* means taking individual rendered frames and turning them into a movie file.

Compositing Your Frames

This procedure uses MPEG Streamclip to composite the rendered frames. MPEG Streamclip is a freeware application that works on both Mac and Windows computers. It's available for download at www.squared5.com/. Follow these steps to perform the compositing:

1. Download, install, and launch MPEG Streamclip. The interface is shown in Figure 14.15.

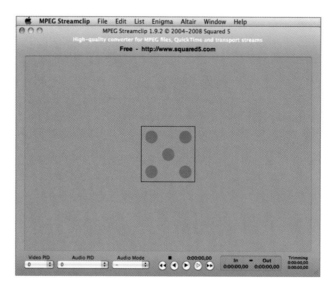

FIGURE 14.15   MPEG Streamclip interface

2. Choose File ➢ Open Files, as shown in Figure 14.16.

FIGURE 14.16
Open Files menu item

3. The Open Files window opens. Change the drop-down list at the bottom of the window to All Files. Navigate to the images directory for your project, and select all the sequentially numbered images in the directory, as shown in Figure 14.17. Click the Open button.

FIGURE 14.17 Selecting the rendered images

4. You may see a File Open Error: Unrecognized File Type alert window. Click the Open Anyway button, shown in Figure 14.18.

FIGURE 14.18 Alert window

5. The frame sequence loads into MPEG Streamclip. To see a playback of your sequence, click one of the playback buttons, shown in Figure 14.19.

Playback buttons

FIGURE 14.19   Playback button locations

6. Choose File ➢ Export To QuickTime, as shown in Figure 14.20.

You can export to AVI if you prefer that format. The steps that follow are the same.

FIGURE 14.20   Export To QuickTime menu item

7. The Movie Exporter window opens. Set Compression to H.264, Quality to 100%, and Frame Rate to 15 fps, as shown in Figure 14.21. Click the Make Movie button.

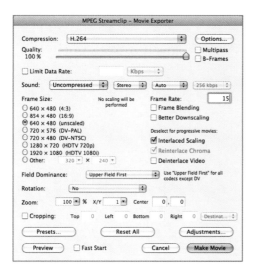

FIGURE 14.21   Movie Exporter window settings

8. The Create New MOV File window opens. Type in a name for your movie, and select a location for the movie to be saved to, as shown in Figure 14.22. The desktop is often a good choice, because it makes the movie easy to find. Click the Save button.

FIGURE 14.22   Create New MOV File window

9. An Export Preview window opens briefly as MPEG Streamclip compiles the movie. When the window closes, your clip is ready for viewing. Navigate to the location where you saved the file, and open it in your player of choice. Figure 14.23 shows the movie opened in QuickTime Player 7. Click Play, and enjoy the results of all your hard work!

FIGURE 14.23   MOV file in a movie player

Using Other Compositing Options

Any software that can create movie files out of individual images can be used to composite rendered frames. Some of these options are listed here:

QuickTime 7 Pro   An upgrade from the QuickTime Player, QuickTime 7 Pro is available from the Apple website and is a handy, simple-to-use compositing tool. Creating a movie in QuickTime 7 Pro is similar to the process you used in MPEG Streamclip. It runs about $30 and is well worth the money.

After Effects   A leading compositing tool published by Adobe, After Effects can do simple composites as well as complex effects. It handles multiple composite layers well and allows you to apply effects and make changes to various aspects of your frames. The learning curve is initially pretty steep, but it's good software to know.

Final Cut/Premiere   Apple's Final Cut (Mac) and Adobe Premiere (PC) are video-editing programs, but they're both capable of loading frame sequences and exporting movie files. Using one of these packages to do a simple composite as you just did is a bit of overkill, but if you know the software and have it available, it's an option.

THE ESSENTIALS AND BEYOND

In this chapter, you created the final version of your character by smoothing the low-resolution mesh, rendered your final frames, and composited the frames into a playable movie file. Your project is complete!

ADDITIONAL EXERCISES

▶ When you applied the smoothing to your character, Maya created a smoothing node at the top of the input stack for the mesh. If you click the model and go to the Channel Box, it's listed as polySmoothFace under the Inputs list. Click polySmoothFace, and the node's channels appear. The Divisions channel is set to 2, the number of divisions you inputted earlier in the chapter. To return your model to its low-resolution state, change 2 to **0**. Divisions can be set as high as 4, although 2 is usually sufficient for a good-looking model.

▶ Try rendering your scene again with a different file type selected for the individual frames, and compare the file sizes and image quality. Targa is a good all-around choice, but sometimes a PNG file or even a JPEG might be a better choice for your project.

Autodesk® Maya® 2014 Certification

Autodesk® certifications are industry-recognized credentials that can help you succeed in your career—providing benefits to both you and your employer. Getting certified is a reliable validation of skills and knowledge, and it can lead to accelerated professional development, improved productivity, and enhanced credibility.

This Autodesk Official Press book can be an effective component of your exam preparation for the Autodesk Maya 2014 Certified Professional exam. Autodesk highly recommends (and we agree!) that you schedule regular time to prepare; review the most current exam preparation roadmap available at www.autodesk.com/certification; use this book; take a class at an Authorized Training Center (find ATCs near you here: www.autodesk.com/atc); and use a variety of resources to prepare for your certification, including plenty of actual hands-on experience.

Certification
Objective

To help you focus your studies on the skills you need for this exam, the following table shows objectives that could potentially appear on an exam and in what chapter you can find information on that topic—and when you go to that chapter, you'll find certification icons like the one in the margin here. This book gives you a foundation for the basic objectives covered in the exam, but you'll need further study and hands-on practice to learn the remaining objectives and complete and pass the Professional exam. For further study, see *Mastering Autodesk Maya 2014* (www.sybex.com/go/masteringmaya2014).

Please refer to www.autodesk.com/certification for the most current exam roadmap and objectives.

Good luck preparing for your certification!

TABLE A.1   Autodesk Maya 2014 Certified Professional exam topics and objectives

Topic	Learning Objective	Chapter
Animation	Analyze the animation of an object using the Graph Editor	Chapter 2
	Constrain an object to a path	Not covered
	Create a path animation and evaluate an object along the path	Not covered
	Edit animation curves using the Graph Editor	Chapter 2
	Identify the constraint used for an animation	Not covered
	List constraint types	Not covered
	Locate the value of keys in the Time Slider	Not covered
	Use animation passes and animation editors	Chapter 2
Cameras	Differentiate camera types	Not covered
	Edit FOV (Field of View)	Chapter 11
	Explain Near and Far Clip Planes for your camera	Not covered
	Identify controls for transforming the camera	Chapter 11
Compositing	Demonstrate how to composite multiple layers together	Not covered

(Continues)

T A B L E   A . 1   *(Continued)*

Topic	Learning Objective	Chapter
Data Management/ Interoperability	Differentiate common file types and usages	Chapter 14
	Use the Import feature to import model data	Not covered
Dynamics/Simulation	Differentiate rigid body dynamics from alternate animation techniques	Not covered
	Explain how to control a soft body simulation	Not covered
	Identify and describe the behavior of a soft body	Not covered
	Identify nConstraint membership properties	Not covered
	Identify rigid body properties	Not covered
	Use soft body simulation tools	Not covered
Effects	Identify an atmosphere effect	Not covered
	Identify an event	Not covered
	Identify and use physical fields	Not covered
	Identify important attributes of OpticalFX	Not covered
	Identify particle render types	Not covered
	Identify particle systems	Not covered
	Use particle system tools	Not covered

(Continues)

TABLE A.1 *(Continued)*

Topic	Learning Objective	Chapter
Lighting	Describe focus attributes on depth map	Not covered
	Differentiate light types	Chapter 13
	Differentiate Depth Map shadows from Raytrace shadows	Chapter 13
	Describe how to use Look Through Selected to place lights in a scene	Chapter 13
	Identify the specular component of a light	Not covered
Materials/Shading	Describe how to fix textures that move on animated/deforming surfaces	Not covered
	Identify how to apply 2D textures	Chapter 6
	List available materials (Blinn, Phong, Lambert)	Not covered
	Indicate the specular shading attributes that are specific to Blinn	Not covered

(Continues)

T A B L E   A . 1 *(Continued)*

Topic	Learning Objective	Chapter
Modeling	Explain the typical workflow for edge loop modeling	Chapter 4
	Identify the typical work-flow for subdivision surface modeling	Not covered
	Identify the type of Boolean operation performed on the objects	Not covered
	Use object creation and modi-fication workflows	Chapters 3, 4, 5
	Use polygon modeling tools	Chapters 3, 4, 5
	Use Boolean	Not covered
Rendering	Describe raytrace/scanline quality settings	Not covered
	List and differentiate renderers	Not covered
	Describe the functionality of render preview within IPR	Chapter 13
	Indicate the rendering set-tings that change when the NTSC preset is enabled	Not covered

(Continues)

TABLE A.1 *(Continued)*

Topic	Learning Objective	Chapter
Rigging/Setup	Describe options for using the Blend Shape deformer	Chapter 8
	Identify bones	Chapter 8
	Identify options for editing rigid skin	Not covered
	Identify options for editing smooth skin	Chapter 9
	Use Weight Table	Not covered
Scene Assembly/ Pipeline Integration	Describe how to import files while preserving scene data	Not covered
	Describe how to improve scene organization by using Search and Rename operations	Not covered
Scripting	Apply (run) scripts	Not covered
	Execute basic scripts	Chapter 5
	Create and run scripts	Chapter 5
	Describe how to add syntax to a script	Not covered
UI/Object Management	Describe and use object transformations	Not covered
	Describe how to display safe frames	Chapter 12
	Describe viewport configuration and ViewCube navigation	Chapter 1
	Identify the purpose and benefits of freezing transformation data on objects	Chapter 10

INDEX

Note to the reader: Throughout this index **boldfaced** page numbers indicate primary discussions of a topic. *Italicized* page numbers indicate illustrations.